Samuel Colt

Samuel Colt

The Man Behind the Gun

By

Colin Holcombe

Front cover image:
Colt's Armoury at Armsmear from across the
Connecticut river.

Back cover image:
Wood engraving
Gunfight with Bank Robbers in a Saloon, 1872

In researching information for this book, I am grateful for the following institutions, organisations and publications:

The Connecticut Historical Society

New England Historical Society

The Society of American Archivists

Wadsworth Atheneum Museum of Art

Click America

NRA. National Firearms Museum of America

San Francisco Sheriff's Department History Online

Alchetron

Publications

Armsmear	Henry Barnard.
Yankee Arms Maker	Jack Rohan
English Pistols and Revolvers	J. N. George
The Book of the Gun	Harold L. Peterson
A History of Firearms	Harold L. Peterson
Samuel Colt's Submarine Battery	Philip Lundeberg
The Devil's Right Hand	William M. Phelps
America's Great Gunmakers	Wayne van Zwoll

Contents

Chapter One

Humble Beginnings

They were hard times towards the turn of the 18th and 19th centuries when Christopher Colt arrived in Hartford Connecticut as a single man from Hadley, Massachusetts. His family were struggling to make a living working on a small farm but having received a fair education and being fed up with living in poverty Christopher had decided to strike out on his own and Hartford seemed to be a thriving town where he could earn a living.

There was a great deal of poverty about and taxpayers were reluctantly having to foot the bill for looking after those who had fallen on hard times. Many were unhappy about having to do so and the law in Connecticut at that time was quite clear, only long-term residents of a community that had fallen on hard times were entitled to any help, a stranger in that position would be, "warned out of town." If anyone ignored the warning to leave and then found themselves in need, they could not expect any help in any form and beggars were thrown into prison, where they would have to work to earn their keep.

The story goes that Christopher, on first arriving in Hartford, and in danger of being "warned out of town," managed to stop a bolting horse and buggy, thus saving the young rider from possible injury or even death.

For this selfless act, good fortune seems to have smiled on the young Christopher that day, for not only did the rider of the horse-drawn buggy turn out to be an attractive young lady, she also happened to be Sarah Caldwell, the daughter of Hartford's richest man, Major John Caldwell.

The frightened but very grateful young Sarah Caldwell persuaded her brave, and she thought, rather handsome young saviour to come home with her to meet her family. Sarah's family were of course all pleased and delighted that she had been delivered from danger and they were suitably impressed by Christopher's bravery. This being the case, he was warmly welcomed into their home and easily persuaded to stay for tea.

When John Caldwell arrived home to see his family entertaining a young stranger he must have been rather surprised. After things had been explained to him, he was of course grateful to the stranger for saving his daughter and the young man in question seemed pleasant enough and to be of good character, but he was not quite as impressed by the young man's feat of bravery as the rest of his family however. The Major was a brave military man who had fought in combat and in the days when horses were more numerous than mobile phones are today, he would have been of the opinion that any physically fit young man should have been capable of stopping a runaway horse pulling a buggy. He was not about to express his opinion openly however when his family, and especially young Sarah, were obviously so taken with the newcomer.

There was an economic boom in Connecticut between 1805 and 1808, brought about mainly by an increase in sea trade, and so, with Major Caldwell giving him support, Colt's fortunes turned and business started to come his way. He also became a frequent visitor to the Caldwell home and began courting Sarah. After a suitable time, he married Sarah Caldwell on April 4th 1805.

Christopher and Sarah had seven children together, four boys and three girls. Two of the girls died in childhood, an all too common occurrence in those days. Sarah Anne, the eldest child was born in 1808, John Caldwell Colt, the eldest boy was born in 1810, Christopher Jr. arrived on the scene in 1812, Samuel Colt was born on July 9th 1814 and James Benjamin, the youngest, put in an appearance in 1816.

Fortunes were being made overnight at this time and Christopher was not one to miss out on a good thing, soon amassing a fortune to rival that of his father-in-law, whom he urged to invest in some of the ventures that were making men rich overnight. The major however, was much more cautious in his business dealings and declined to get involved in what he saw as, get rich quick, enterprises and in the end, he was proved right.

In 1807, the Embargo Act caused prices to tumble and newly made millionaires were made penniless even more quickly than they had become rich. This act was a general embargo on all foreign nations enacted by the United States Congress against Great Britain and France during the Napoleonic Wars.

The act was introduced in response to American merchant ships and their cargo being seized as contraband of war by European navies. Britain even resorted to "Impressment" forcing thousands of Americans, who had been born in Britain, into service on British warships. President Thomas Jefferson however, resisted calls for a declaration of war, instead arguing for commercial warfare. The Embargo Act was expected to bring economic hardship to the waring nations but instead, it inflicted huge burdens on the United States economy and the American people. It had the effect of simultaneously undermining American citizens' faith that their government could execute its own laws fairly, and strengthening the conviction among America's enemies, that its republican form of government didn't work. After just 15 months, the Embargo Act was revoked on March 1, 1809, during the last days of Jefferson's presidency. The tension with

Britain continued to grow however, eventually leading to the War of 1812.

President Thomas Jefferson

Christopher, like so many others, had overstretched himself financially and was one of those to see his fortune disappear like water down a drain. He survived only because his father-in-law was able to help him out.

The experience taught Christopher an important lesson however and he would never again spend money that he didn't actually have. The major, perhaps believing that the time when he would meet his maker was not far off, summoned his lawyer and divided his fortune into trust funds for each of his children.

Sarah, who was used to living the life of a wealthy woman, continued to spoil her children, even when her husband hit financial troubles and eventually became bankrupt. She was also in poor health by then, suffering from consumption (pulmonary tuberculosis) to which she eventually succumbed and died on 16th June 1821. Having loved her children so much, it is perhaps a blessing that she didn't live to see Sarah Anne, who became depressed by having to live in what she regarded as virtual poverty, commit suicide at the age of just twenty-one,

Christopher was in despair, a bankrupt with children to raise, he had now lost both the love of his life and the income from her trust fund, that was now taken out of his hands and doled out by the trustees only for the needs of the children. He needed help. His widowed sister, Aunt Price, who kept house for him, was as indulgent with the children as Sarah had been and things were going from bad to worse.

Eventually help came in the form of a new wife, Olive Sargeant, the daughter of a well to do mechanic whom he married in 1823.

Olive was a born manager and she got a firm grip on the family finances straight away, she drastically reduced the family outgoings and all unnecessary expenditure was stopped, something that did not sit well with the children, or Aunt Price who always sided with them. There were constant rows and disagreements in the family about money. Olive was the one in charge however and she was determined that what money they did have coming in, would not only have to support the family but would also go towards restoring Christopher's business standing

Olive tried her best to reconcile the family to a more frugal lifestyle but eventually she had to concede defeat and took drastic action. Aunt Price was dismissed, John was sent off to live with an uncle who apprenticed him to the bookkeeper of the Union Manufacturing Company in Marlboro, Massachusetts. Sarah Anne was sent to another relative, Samuel was indentured for a year to a farmer at Glastonbury, on the understanding that he was to do the household chores and attend Glastonbury school. Christopher Jr. had worked up a small business getting orders for local traders and was allowed to stay at the family home with James, who was still under six years of age.

It's unclear whether Samuel enjoyed working on a farm or not. He was now eleven years old and it was probably around this time that he became interested in science and engineering, preferring to read about those subjects rather than his bible studies or doing chores around the house.

Many accounts of his life at this time tell that Samuel had a pistol with him when he went to the farm, but if he did, it is unclear how he came by it, and he would certainly have kept its existence a secret from both his father and step-mother and the farmer, although his mother Sarah, coming from a military background would have had no problems with her son owning a firearm, some even suggest that she was the one who gave it to him.

It is known that when his brother John was seven years of age and loved to play at soldiers, Sarah had supplied him with a military uniform, small rifles and a small brass cannon. It was only after the cannon blew up one day, that his father banned the children from having anything to do with firearms of any sort

Samuel did manage to acquire himself some free time on the farm once he had completed his chores, which included, cutting firewood, watering and feeding the stock, clearing paths and helping with milking.

He is reputed to have read avidly at these time from his, *Compendium of Knowledge*. It was from that book that he learned of various inventors and the wonderful things they had achieved, sometimes changing the way things were done forever.

At some point, he came across articles about Robert Fulton and his work on developing a submarine and torpedoes for Napoleon. In 1800, Fulton had produced the "Nautilus," widely accepted as the world's first practical submarine. Fulton is also credited with inventing some of the world's earliest naval torpedoes for use by the British Royal Navy.

These articles were to set the young Samuel Colt on a course. He was determined to make his fortune by becoming an inventor like Robert Fulton.

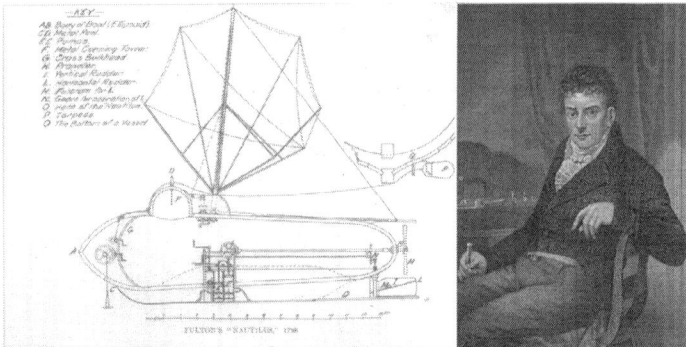

Robert Fulton and a drawing of his "Nautilus"

In 1829, Samuel's year at the farm was over and so at the age of fifteen he returned home and his father sent him to begin work at the textile plant, he had just established in Ware,

Massachusetts. Exposed at his father's factory to chemicals, tools and materials, as well a deep well of knowledge and expertise from the plant's workforce, Samuel must have been overjoyed, here he was in his element and he could begin his work as an inventor.

No doubt referring once again to his encyclopaedia, the *Compendium of Knowledge*, Samuel built a homemade galvanic cell and after some experiments to prove that he could set off an explosive charge using an electric current from it, he had hand-bills printed and circulated, declaring that on the Fourth of July, he would explode a raft on Ware Pond, using underwater explosives.

Samuel's idea was to detonate the explosives under the raft by means of an electric current and that this current would be delivered to the explosives by means on an underwater cable that he would protect from the water by wrapping it in tar-soaked cloth.

One can imagine the scene on the day, with an expectant crowed gathered around the pond to witness the raft being blown up, all dressed in their Sunday best for the Fourth of July celebrations. Well, there was indeed an explosion, but things didn't go entirely to Samuel's plan, the raft had drifted from its moorings and was no longer in place above the explosives. All the explosion achieved was to send a water spout into the air and cover many of those watching in mud and dirty water.

Furious, and no doubt feeling that they had been the victims of a deliberate prank, an angry mob went in search of Samuel, who had to flee or almost certainly suffer a beating.

Samuel was reputedly aided in his escape from the crowd by one Elisha K. Root, a young mechanic who had come to Ware from Chicopee Falls, specifically to witness the demonstration.

Root was also an inventor and realised that Samuel had set off the charge using an electric spark and he wanted to know how he had delivered the spark through the water. Samuel, although grateful for Root's help in escaping the mob, was not ready to share and kept his secret, explaining to Root that he intended to make his living by inventing things and could not therefore give up the secret.

The two young men hit it off straight away and during their long conversation, Root explained to Samuel the practise of first making detailed drawings of his mechanical ideas and then wooden models, before making the actual thing itself. Advice that the young Samuel would remember.

Events in Hartford saved the people of Ware the trouble of taking action against Samuel. Sarah Anne, just twenty-one years of age, had found living in what she regarded as abject poverty intolerable and she killed herself by taking poison.

John, at around the same time, ran away from Marlboro and joined the Marine Corps. Christopher Jr. had gone off on his own as a small merchant, leaving only James the youngest at home. Olive was fearful that people would seek revenge on Samuel for his supposed "prank" and persuaded his father to take him out of the factory and send him to Amherst Academy for schooling.

Samuel was far from pleased to be taken away from the factory and sent to college but knew that he had no choice but to comply. Once there, he immediately felt an outsider, the hierarchy amongst his fellow students was largely determined by sporting and athletic prowess and Samuel knew nothing of games or sport and had no desire to learn.

He did gradually build a small following among some of his fellow students however, by demonstrating his underwater mine on a small scale and making firecrackers, which often got him into trouble with the school authorities. On July 4th 1830, an accident with one of his fireworks resulted in a small fire that damaged some college property. While the college authorities were considering what his fate should be, Samuel packed his bags and made his way home to Hartford.

Chapter Two

All at Sea

One can only imagine Christopher's disappointment when his son returned home from Amherst and the discussions must have been heated to say the least but in the end, Christopher conceded that Samuel had worked well at Glastonbury and at Ware and had not asked to be sent to Amherst, but there was still the problem of what to do with him.

After much discussion, it was decided that Samuel should go to sea and learn the trade of a mariner. Samuel himself actually had no more desire for a life at sea than he had for life on a farm or an education at Amherst Academy, but once again he found himself faced with a fait accompli.

Christopher apprenticed Samuel to a Captain Spaulding of the brig, Corlo, which was sailing from Boston on a voyage to Calcutta, India, and back carrying both goods and some missionaries.

Samuel Lawrence of the Boston firm Lawrence and Stone, outfitted Samuel for the voyage and the itemised bill dated 2nd August 1830, comprised the following:

Seaman's cap	$ 3.50
Quadrant, almanac and compass	18.50
Mattress and bedding	9.00
Slop Clothes	38.92
Boots and shoes	8.00
Stockings	2.00
Jack-knife	1.00
Custom House	.25
Seaman's Chest	4.62
	$85.79
Cash	5.00
Paper & C	.45
Total	$91.24

With the bill Lawrence wrote a note to Christopher saying, *"Above is a memorandum of the sums paid for your son. It was necessary to be prepared for cold and warm weather, and in a fitting out there are a great many things necessary which need not be replaced for years. Sam will not require any money of consequence; he may find something to bring home. I told the supercargo to advance him fifty dollars if he requires it. The ship sailed this morning. The last time I saw Sam he was in tarpaulin, checked shirt, checked trousers, on the fore-topsail yard, loosing the topsail. He is a manly fellow, and I have no doubt will do credit to all concerned. He was in good spirits on departure. There were some thousand present to see the missionaries off. Prayers and singing were performed on board."*

There is nothing in the records to show that Samuel had any contact with the missionaries whilst on board other than in a brief reference to them in a letter to his father in which he states, *"Since we have missionaries aboard, Aunt Price probably will feel perfectly easy for me."*

Life at sea on a sailing ship in those days was no picnic, discipline was strict and punishments harsh and Samuel must have wondered why any man would choose such a life. When weather conditions were bad, every member of the crew was rushed off their feet and there was little time for sleep, but when the weather was calm, there were occasions when they could enjoy some small amount of leisure time.

When he had first stepped aboard the Corlo, Samuel had been asked as a matter of routine, if he had any weapons on his person and he had proudly shown his pistol, but pride had turned to dismay as it was confiscated, to be returned only after the voyage was over. It was explained to Samuel that only officers were allowed firearms on board. At first, Samuel thought it was a great injustice that only a certain class were allowed firearms but during the course of the voyage, he witnessed first-hand how the strict rules and harsh discipline were at times very necessary. Men were sometimes hit to stir them into action quickly and this could be resented by the crew and lead to the possibility of conflict between officers and men, a situation that could easily jeopardise the safety of the entire ship.

It is often stated in books on Colt's life, that it was while enjoying some leisure time and observing the ship's wheel, that Colt got the idea for his revolver. Whichever way the wheel was turned, a spoke was always lined up with a clutch that could be set to hold it in place. This may or may not have been the case, but it is certainly how Samuel himself said he came up with the idea for his revolver.

In many books where this anecdote is described, however, the reader could be forgiven for thinking that the idea of a repeating arm, utilising a revolving cylinder, was a completely new idea, but the truth is that revolver pistols not only, already existed but had done so for many years. Samuel Colt did not invent the revolver, he did however, greatly improve its design.

Colt himself would have been more than familiar with the pepperbox revolvers of the time, that were the most popular form of personal defence, and with the operation of the various types of machinery at his father's factory, a keen engineering mind like his could easily have devised a system for revolving the cylinder of a gun as it was being cocked and securing it in place for firing, which were the two principle improvements Colt came up with.

The pepperbox revolvers of the time mostly had the cylinders rotated manually after each firing and there was no device to lock the cylinder in place for firing, resolving these shortcomings and the addition a single barrel were the main improvements in Colt's design.

There is little doubt that it was on this voyage, that he came up with a definite design for his gun, even if not the basic idea, and possibly with Elisha K. Root's words still fresh in mind, and having observed seaman whittling wood with their knives, he carved a wooden pattern of it during leisure moments.

Samuel's disliking for the sea increased the more time he spent on it and the fact that he didn't sign on with Captain Spaulding for a second voyage didn't go down too well. Spaulding saw Samuel's refusal to sign on again as a personal afront and wrote to the boy's father.

Christopher Colt was equally dismayed when he learned of his son's decision to abandon the sea, saying that in that case, his expenditure on Samuel had been a complete waste of money, but Samuel stood his ground this time, and explained to his father that his time at sea had not been wasted at all, because it had given him the time to invent a revolver that was far better than anything that had gone before, and that with it he would make his fortune.

To back up his claim, Samuel showed his father the wooden model of the gun he had made and explained its operation. His father must have been suitably impressed by both the model and Samuel's description of how it would operate, because Christopher agreed to finance the making of two guns, as well as the necessary patents if the pistols performed as Samuel insisted they would. In the meantime, Samuel was to return to work at his father's textile factory in Ware.

Samuel was of course delighted with his father's decision but he stipulated that his father should search for and employ, only the best gunsmith available.

Christopher set out to find a suitable gunsmith with almost as much enthusiasm in the project as his son, but it was during Christopher's search for such gunsmith, that his enthusiasm for his son's gun began to ebb. Several of the gunsmiths he approached cast doubt on whether the pistol would actually work. He was also dismayed by the cost of employing a competent gunsmith, they certainly didn't come cheap. Christopher was a man of his word, however, and although he no longer had confidence in his son's invention, he had agreed to finance the making of two and he would not renege on a promise.

He would keep his word and have two guns made but he saw no reason to pay over the odds for them, so he decided that an ordinary mechanic, rather than a qualified gunsmith, would be just as up to the task of making them.

He decided not to tell Samuel about his change of heart however, thinking perhaps, that if the boy found out for himself that his idea was no good, he would give up the idea of becoming an inventor and pursue a more conventional career.

Working back at his father's textile factory in Ware, whilst anxiously waiting for his guns to be made, Samuel spent time assisting one William Smith, a chemist who was in charge of the bleaching and dyeing department. Samuel had become a keen amateur scientist and under the tutelage of William Smith learned something of chemistry and became somewhat of an authority on nitrous oxide (laughing-gas.)

The world at that time knew very little of the gas and Samuel and William tried it out on each other and found the effects to be both harmless and amusing.

In fact, the gas was first synthesised in 1772 by English natural philosopher and chemist Joseph Priestley, who called it phlogisticated nitrous air. The first practical use of the gas was made by Thomas Beddoes and James Watt who jointly published a book entitled, "Considerations on the Medical Use and on the Production of Factitious Airs," in 1794.

Clinical trials started in 1798 when Thomas Beddoes established a, Pneumatic Institution for Relieving Diseases by Medical Airs, in Hotwells in Bristol, England, under the supervision of a young Humphrey Davy. Davy discovered that inhalation of nitrous oxide could relieve a person of pain, but despite his discovery, it was another forty-four years before doctors used it for anaesthesia.

Early in 1832, Christopher notified Samuel that the revolvers were finished and ready for testing but now being sceptical of their worth, cautioned him that he doubted they would work.

When Samuel arrived home and examined the guns for himself, he was mortified. The workmanship was crude and badly finished and the fitting was poor.

Samuel knew that a poorly made gun was just as much a danger to the shooter as it was to the intended target. In fact, he was so worried when he saw the guns, that he clamped them to a vice for the test firing and pulled the triggers with a cord from a distance. One gun failed to fire at all and the other burst on its first firing and would surely have caused injury had

Samuel not taken the precautions he had.

Upset and annoyed, Samuel complained bitterly that his pistols hadn't been properly made and therefore hadn't been given a fair trial, but his father told him of the opinions expressed by some of the various gunsmiths he'd spoken to.

Samuel was furious and pointed out that it wasn't the opinions of the gunsmiths that were needed, it was their skill and workmanship.

Humphrey Davy 1778 -1829 English chemist and inventor President of the Royal Society and inventor of the Davy safety lamp

Thomas Beddoes 1760-1808 English physician and scientific writer who worked to treat tuberculosis

His father nevertheless insisted that Samuel return to work with William Smith, from whom he had heard good things of Samuel, and Samuel, not for the first time in his life, felt he had little choice but to comply, declaring however, that he would not rest until his invention had been given a fair trial.

With his bitterness increasing as the weeks went by, Samuel strived to save enough money from his wages to pay for a competent gunsmith but very soon realised that it would take him years to save so much.

He racked his brains to come up with some way of making money quickly and finally he hit upon the idea of using his new found knowledge of nitrous oxide to that end. He would put together a sideshow, demonstrating the effects of the gas to the general public, who would no doubt pay to be both entertained and educated by the spectacle.

Giving his father no inkling of what he was planning, knowing instinctively that any such plan would meet with parental disapproval, he assembled a portable laboratory on a handcart to produce the nitrous oxide gas.

We have no idea what Samuel's apparatus looked like or just how he administered the gas but Humphry Davy's method of production was to gently heat ammonium nitrate to decompose it into nitrous oxide and water vapour. The ammonium nitrate had to be heated to between 170°C and

240°C because higher temperatures could cause the ammonium nitrate to explode. The next step is to cool the gases to condense the water and this is achieved by use of a pneumatic trough and bubbling the gases up through water into a collecting jar.

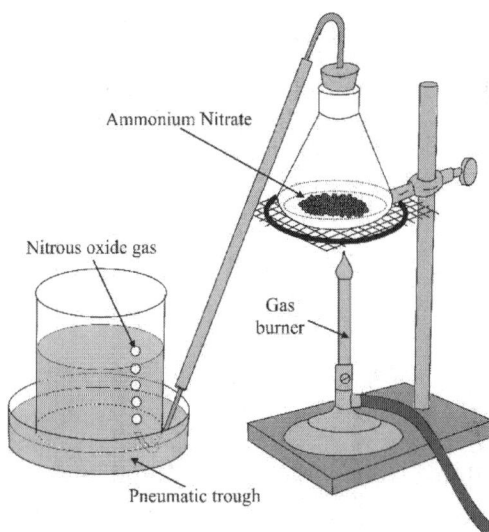

Method of producing nitrous oxide gas

It is unclear whether Samuel took William Smith into his confidence about his intentions, or whether he kept him in the dark, worried that William might lose his job if his father thought they had colluded together.

After dropping his father a line, simply stating that he was off to earn his fortune, he set off on a tour of the villages around Ware, setting up his equipment on the village greens or commons and demonstrating the effects of the gas, at first on himself and then on those spectators willing to try it for themselves. While the volunteers who inhaled the gas amused the crowds, Samuel took up a collection and business was good.

Soon however, the size of the crowds turning up for Samuel's demonstrations began to tail off.

Church attendance had been at an all-time low following the American Revolution but over the first part of the nineteenth century, Americans began joining churches and religious organizations with unprecedented enthusiasm as a series of religious revivals, collectively known as the "Second Great Awakening," swept the nation. Beginning on the western frontier and spreading both north and south, the awakening produced thousands of new church going protestants.

Evangelical Protestantism surged to the forefront of cultural and social influence across America in the 1820s and 1830s, as wealthy businessmen and influential families of the Northeast, increasingly brought their faith to bear upon public life. Frivolous entertainment such as theatrical performance was frowned upon and although Samuel's one-man show was a harmless, arguably scientific demonstration, it was still theatre to the masses and the church's disapproval was reducing the size of his audiences.

1840s wood engraving showing two men inhaling
Nitrous Oxide Gas

To remedy the situation, Samuel removed all mention of entertainment from his handbills and fliers, content to let his customers discover for themselves that the demonstration was amusing and entertaining.

His business improved when the clergy no longer objected to his activities and he began to average around ten dollars a day, more than ten times what he could have expected to earn in any kind of paid employment.

As soon as he had enough money put aside, he travelled to Washington and deposited a description of his invention in the Patent Office.

Samuel then wrote to his father and revealed to him for the first time the manner in which he had been making his living. Samuel knew of course that his father would not approve, he would not be fooled by Samuel referring to a side-show as a scientific lecture but he also took the opportunity to have a bit of a dig at his father, saying that he was now making arrangements for the construction of properly made pistols by skilled craftsmen.

Samuel's father was away on business when his letter arrived and it was opened by Olive. James was unable to make out what their step-mother thought of the letter and, as far as we know, neither she nor Christopher ever spoke of Samuel's time on the road as a showman.

Samuel arranged to have two revolvers made, with an agreement that permitted him to pay for the work in instalments. He gave a number of performances of his show in small towns around Baltimore and then went on to Boston, determined to elevate his show from street corners and village greens to theatres and public halls.

Within just a couple of months of leaving Ware he was knocking on the doors of libraries, museums and other places of learning, to book space for his scientific demonstration of the wonderous effects of Nitrous Oxide Gas.

Although still not quite eighteen, he must have cut a striking figure of a man in a frock coat and high hat while sporting an impressive beard and moustache, he would have looked just what his handbills claimed him to be, "The Celebrated Dr. Coult of New York, London and Calcutta."

Samuel never explained why he changed the spelling of his name for his performances and he never used it in any of his private correspondence. It may be that even then, he was convinced that he would one day be a prominent figure in business and didn't want the name Colt to be associated with a common side-show entertainer.

The Boston Masonic Temple was host to all the more important lectures and exhibitions of the day, and even a sparsely attended meeting there would gain him some much-needed prestige, so it was there that he set his sights. Having booked the Temple for a two-day engagement, he spent all the money that he had left, on advertising space in the Boston papers and having handbills printed.

He gambled that, even if he did badly, he would still take enough in ticket sales to cover his expenses and get him to his next port of call. He had also invested in a silver embroidered black drape to cover the table his apparatus rested on and a stout net to stretch across the front of the stage to stop anyone that had inhaled the gas from taking an unwanted dive into the orchestra pit.

The Masonic Temple was crowded on both nights and the takings far exceeded his most optimistic expectations. However, despite his lavish advertising outlay, the local press had let him down. On the morning of the 22nd June 1832 the Boston Morning Post gave only a few lines to the performance and the name of Dr. Coult was not even mentioned.

The Post's notice read, "*The exhibition of the singular and amusing effects of nitrous oxide gas, when inhaled into the lungs, will be repeated, this evening only, at the Masonic Temple. (See Advertisement)*"

Samuel had been hoping for good notices that he could cut out and use to advertise successive shows. He complained bitterly to the editors that he had only spent the amount of money he had with them, in order to gain notices.

They replied that they had no idea that had been his intention and that if they had, they would have declined to print the advertisements, saying that there was no way they could treat his obviously clowning performance, either as science or as a dramatic art.

After his experience in Boston, Samuel had learnt his lesson and made sure that when placing advertisements for his shows in future, such as the one recreated here from the Albany Gazette in 1833, that the editors were in no doubt about what he expected from them.

Albany Museum

Nitrous Oxide Gas, For Monday, Tuesday and Wednesday Evenings, Oct. 28, 29, 30.

The proprietors of the Museum, at the earnest solicitations of a number of patrons who have not had an opportunity of witnessing the interesting effects of the Nitrous Oxide or Exhilarating Gas during Dr. COULT'S previous exhibition, have made arrangements with him to exhibit, for three nights only, in the lecture room of the Museum.

The peculiar effect of this singular compound upon the animal system, was first noticed by Sir Humphry Davy. He observed that when inhaled into the lungs, it producing the most astonishing effects on the nervous system, that some individuals were disposed to laugh, sing and dance; others to recitation and declamation, and that the greater number had an irresistible propensity to muscular exertion, such as wrestling, boxing and other innumerable fantastic feats. In short, the sensation produced by it are highly pleasurable and are not followed by debility.

Dr. Coult, being a practiced chemist, no fears need be entertained of inhaling an impure gas, and he is willing to submit his preparations to the inspection of any scientific gentleman.

Dr. Coult, has exhibited the extraordinary powers of this gas in many cities of the U. States, to numerous audiences of ladies and gentlemen of the first respectability, when many ladies inhaled the gas. Those ladies who may be desirous of witnessing its extortionary powers, are assured that the house enables every accommodation for their comfort, and that not any shadow of impropriety attends the exhibition.

N.B. Those persons who inhale the gas will be separated from the audience by means of a net, so that the spectators will have a chance to see their performance and will be perfectly free from danger.

Exhibition to commence at 8 ½ O'clock.

Admittance 25 cents.

This new approach seemed to work, at least if the notice in the Albany Microscope is anything to go by, it read, *"We never beheld such an anxiety as there has been during the past week to witness the astonishing effects of Dr. Coult's gas. The Museum was crowded to excess every evening; and so intense the interest which was manifest, that the doctor has been compelled to give two exhibitions almost every evening.*

"The effect which the gas produces upon the system is truly astonishing. The person who inhales it becomes completely insensible, and remains in that state for about the space of three minutes, when his senses become restored, and he sneaks off with as much shame as if he had been guilty of some mean action.

"No person will begrudge his two shillings for the gratification of half an hour's laugh at the ludicrous feats displayed in the lecture room."

At some time, Samuel received a letter from his brother John, inviting him to bring his show to Cincinnati, and it held out the promise, not only of, "large profits with which to lay the foundations of his fortune, but of fun and frolic as well."

Samuel was delighted at the prospect of, not just taking his show to Cincinnati, but of visiting his brother John, of whom he was very fond.

Chapter Three

Brother John

John Colt you'll remember had been sent off to live with an uncle who apprenticed him to the bookkeeper of the Union Manufacturing Company in Marlboro, Massachusetts.

John however, was too fond of adventure and fun to live his life as a bookkeeper, so he ran away from Marlboro and after some time drifting around the country, he reached the Ohio River. Here he found a job as a cabin boy on one of the river boats.

Life on the riverboats was fun but it failed to satisfy his longing for adventure. He tried lying about his age in order to join the United States Marine Corps but failed. The corps only accepted minors with the written and notarized consent of a parent or guardian and it would appear that in the end, John somehow managed to persuade his father to give his consent, in order for him to join. Christopher probably thought the discipline of the corps would do the boy some good.

John immediately threw himself into the military life with a passion. He was painstaking in the performance of his duties and hungry to acquire the kind of knowledge that would make him a better soldier. He worked and studied hard and soon won the regard of his officers, if not his comrades, who regarded him as something of a teacher's pet.

He was so disliked by his comrades in fact, that many of them tried to take him on physically, but those who did soon discovered that they had bitten off more than they could chew, John was well able to take care of himself in a fight.

When a vacancy occurred among the corporals, although it was against custom to promote a marine with such short service, John's record was so outstanding that he was given the rank without question, and he wore the chevrons with enormous pride.

It would seem that John's arrogant and overbearing nature, that had been a handicap to him in civilian life, was an asset to him as a non-commissioned officer. He loved being in command, military discipline was his god and he soon whipped his squad into shape.

It was inevitable that his promotion to sergeant would soon follow and when it did, he performed so well in that position that he was quickly promoted to the post of "first sergeant," over the heads of others that had been in the rank far longer. John fitted into the military life so well in fact, that his captain began coaching him for a commission and his future in the military seemed to be heading ever upwards.

Who knows how John's life would have turned out if

he had stayed in the military, certainly, a very unpleasant episode in the history of the Colt family would have been avoided, but more of that later.

Just what was going on in John's head we will never know, but it is clear that for some reason his enthusiasm for the military life faded and he wanted desperately to get out of the Marine Corps.

He had no intention of deserting however, he knew only too well that those who did were ruthlessly hunted down and punished, so he turned his mind to ways of escaping the corps without leaving a stain on his military career.

John had enlisted as a minor, so his father had the right to claim his discharge, but when John wrote to his father asking him to do so, his father refused. Christopher regarded it as a matter of honour that John should complete his term of enlistment and advised his son that, with application and hard work, he could undoubtedly win a commission and do well for himself in the service.

John was not interested in advice, all he wanted from his father was a means of quitting the corps without a stain on his record. To this end John used his skilful penmanship to forge his father's handwriting and draft a letter to say that his father was desperately ill and needed his son to get out of the Marine Corps and come home without delay.

John's Captain, thinking that John must be dismayed by his father's request, told him not to worry and that only a definite demand from his father, that he dared not ignore, would cause him to release John, so for a while at least, John was stuck.

John, even as a child, had been good at copying his father's handwriting, so after a sufficient interval of time, in order to eliminate any suspicion, he composed another letter, one that his captain could not ignore and sent it to James at Hartford, to be posted from there.

When his captain told John the "bad news" he was still willing to write to Christopher on John's behalf and it was only the belief that Christopher was too ill to be open to reason that prevented him from doing so. John was given his discharge and assured that when his father recovered from his illness he could return to the Corps and a good berth would be found for him.

Once free of the service and its life of discipline, John turned to the Mississippi and a carefree life on the river boats. He relied on his wits and lived the life of a gambler. With a little money in his pocket there was always the chance of winning a fortune on the turn of a card. His luck eluded him on the Mississippi however and he turned to the Ohio, but he fared no better there. There was a slump in commodity prices and the wealthy plantation owners were off trying to extend their loans rather than trying their luck at the tables.

John then turned his back on the river and looked ashore to Cincinnati with its pleasant climate and wealthy citizens. These citizens took pride in the beauty and culture of their city and encouraged the social graces. The city had both an art school and a gallery, along with a Museum that combined the features of a theatre, opera house and concert hall. Local talent was encouraged and artists, musicians and actors from all over were frequent visitors.

John fell in a group living a Bohemian lifestyle and after a while became romantically involved with a young slave girl, who was also the mistress of her owner. Between trips on the river to replenish his purse, John devoted all his time to her and the couple became so enamoured of each other that they threw discretion to the wind and their affair became common knowledge.

Eventually the girl's owner learned of the affair and took his revenge, he stripped her of her fine clothes and belongings and sent her south to work in the fields with the other slaves to atone for her ungrateful and disrespectful behaviour.

John returned from one of his river trips and was dismayed to find the girl gone. After searching desperately for her he eventually learned the truth and challenged her owner to a duel, but his challenge was contemptuously rejected. Gentlemen of the south did not fight duels with river rats he was told and if he made any kind of hostile move, he would be shot like the dog he was. John was angry and upset at losing the love of his life and found no comfort in the fact that public opinion would be firmly on the side of the girl's owner, and that even if he found and married her, the law would have her returned to her owner.

John grieved the loss of his love for a while but then took up with another beauty, a singer, who was by all accounts so fair of face that apparently, men failed to notice that she had an unpleasant speaking voice and sang off key. Women however, immune to her beauty, did pick up on the singer's defects, a fact that seriously affected her managers income and she found herself stranded in Cincinnati.

To keep such a beautiful woman in a fitting style John had to make frequent trips to the river to replenish his coffers, but one time when he returned, after a particularly long string of good luck, he once again found the love of his life departed. Apparently, during his absence the lady had found a manager willing to overlook her shortcomings and finance her career, so she had left with him for New Orleans.

John had now had his fill of the Bohemian life and

sought a career that would give his domestic life more stability. Whilst in the Marine Corps, John had completed his knowledge of bookkeeping, so living on the funds from his recent run of good luck, he compiled a textbook on the subject of double entry book-keeping and published it as the work of a "former government official." The idea of double entry book-keeping had been around since the 1200s but John's book, "*The Science of Double entry Book-Keeping,*" explained it in a simple and innovative way, making it a great success.

Encouraged by the success of the book, he started a school of accounting and when that proved profitable, he established a correspondence school of business, which may well have been the first in the country, if not the world.

In spite of the wild oats he had sown, John now seemed destined for a life of wealth and respectability as an esteemed author and educator. But although his days were taken up with business, his nights saw him returning to his old haunts and it was inevitable that he would embark on another love affair, this time with a married woman.

His new love was an actress who appeared in an acrobatic singing comedy with her husband. As a handsome ex-marine, John had little difficulty in winning the lady's affections, but her husband was in John's eyes, "unreasonable" about the whole thing and made trouble.

The Museum where his new lover's the act was performing was in financial difficulties and John, using his prestige as a business teacher, persuaded the owners to hire him as manager. His first action as manager of the theatre was to cancel his new lady-friend's booking.

The husband, now unable to support his wife, could do little as she and John set up house together. The house they shared became a rendezvous centre for aspiring artists and actors such as the struggling young sculptor, Hiram Powers, who later became known internationally, not least for his sculpture of a Greek slave shown here, and the actor and playwright John Howard Payne, best remembered for writing, "Home Sweet Home."

Being the generous host was an expensive business but it gained John a large circle of friends, some of who were destined to become famous.

John's house was packed with party goers when Samuel arrived and he was pleased to see his brother displaying all the signs of wealth and prosperity. He couldn't have been happier, surely his wealthy brother would be willing to advance him the money needed to complete the development of his pistol, obtain the patents and launch his business.

It didn't take Samuel long to discover however, that his brother was spending his money as quickly as he was earning it and was even getting into debt. Samuel urged John to bring an end to the constant entertaining and open house lifestyle but his advice fell on deaf ears.

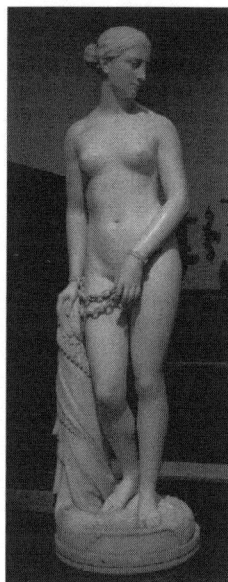

Hiram Powers 1805 – 1873
American neoclassical sculptor, he was one of the first American artists to gain international acclaim, largely based on his sculpture of a Greek slave, shown here.

Samuel struck up a friendship at this time with Hiram Powers, who was financing his study of sculpture by modelling puppets and giving shows with them. Powers had been trying to perfect a pyrotechnic spectacle which he purposed to call "The Infernal Regions," but he had been unable to develop satisfactory fireworks. Samuel solved that problem for him and the two men formed a partnership, combining the nitrous oxide induced comedy of Dr. Coult and the Faustian tragedies of Power's puppets.

Their combined efforts packed the Museum to capacity every night and John was delighted, fully expecting the show to run for a year or more. Samuel, however, was much more realistic about the show's prospects. He deduced from careful observation of the audiences, that few locals would attend the show more than once and when they had all seen it, there were too few visitors to Cincinnati to keep it going.

Because of this, Samuel constantly changed the firework displays in the "Infernal Regions" part of the show and introduced novelties into his nitrous oxide demonstrations.

On one occasion, he hired six Native Americans to appear in his gas act and advertised it widely. The performance was packed that night but the audience was intensely nervous, many of them expecting trouble and carrying stout sticks and in some cases small derringer pistols.

The Native Americans, having inhaled the gas, proceeded to go sound asleep without even a giggle, let alone the much-expected war-dance.

Poor Samuel was aghast, this was not what his patrons had come to see, but he was the master of thinking on his feet and turning to his audience, as if this was just what was expected, he announced that the next part of the show would be to see just who, under influence of the gas, would be inspired to wake the sleeping braves.

A large blacksmith mounted the stage and inhaled almost the entire contents of the gasbag in a single breath. Samuel tried to snatch the bag from him as he prepared to take another breath, but he failed in his attempt and after inhaling once more, the blacksmith tossed the bag aside and made a grab for Samuel, who deftly skipped away.

Samuel dodged around the stage for several minutes perused by the now bellowing blacksmith as the Museum was rocked by applause and laughter. Samuel eventually escaped his pursuer, who toppled into the sleepers, knocking them off their chairs before starting an oration. After a few moments, he stopped mid-sentence as the effects of the gas wore off, then stood incoherent for a moment, before shamefacedly returning to his seat while the audience howled their approval, and the Native Americans looked about, wondering what on earth had been happening.

The general opinion was that Samuel had planned the whole thing and was credited with being the most outstanding showman. The ever practical Samuel however, realised that the shows were far too unpredictable an enterprise on which to build a fortune, he needed to build and sell his guns.

He was living well and had a good social life and there was certainly no lack of female companionship. The show was making good money but after advertising, the cost of props and paying rent to the Museum, the net profits were little better than his street corner days.

Chapter Four

Cholera scare

Samuels intention on leaving Cincinnati was to travel to the cities he considered most likely to supply him with packed houses for his demonstrations but progress on the Ohio river was slow with the steamers stopping, not just at every landing but also when being hailed from the bank.

Mississippi river steamboats

Samuel was more than willing to demonstrate his nitrous oxide gas to anyone that could pay his price and he was surprised to find that that many of the slaves he encountered could produce two shillings, just as readily as their owners, but it was not the done thing for a white man to entertain slaves directly. It was alright if a slave owner paid him to entertain his slaves but not for the slaves to pay him direct.

Once he entered the Mississippi things changed however, the abolitionist sentiment of Ohio, Indiana and Illinois, that sought to ease the lot of the slave, did not extend below the Ohio River.

Writing home to his father and speaking of the trade and ownership of slaves, Samuel did not express any particular revulsion at their treatment, treatment that the abolitionists constantly denounced as unchristian, but merely stated that slavery was a *"great nuisance."*

What was the point of directing and instructing an unwilling slave to perform a task that could more easily and quickly be achieved by oneself? He would have much preferred to set up his own apparatus in the New Orleans Opera House, but the customs and prejudices of the place made it necessary to use slaves. How the South could keep going with such a wasteful, inefficient and generally unsatisfactory system of labour was beyond Samuel's understanding.

"I deem it to have a bad effect on the white people themselves," he wrote, *"not only do they grow up incapable of doing for themselves even the smallest service, so accustomed*

are they to having everything done for them, but they are so used to lording it over their chattels that they frequently conduct themselves with their equals in such arrogant fashion as to give offence constantly."

"Many intelligent Southerners think as I do. They hold it would be a blessing if all the slaves could be shipped back to Africa tomorrow and not a slave left in the country. But of course, it cannot be done. The traders in slaves and their bankers make a great deal of money out of it and would oppose any change. The planters are so much in debt to these, I am told, that they could not get rid of the slaves without their consent."

It would seem that slavery was not a problem with which Samuel troubled to wrestle at that time, especially as he was doing so well himself. New Orleans had been profitable and he would have stayed longer if there hadn't been a general exodus from the city because of a cholera scare.

Samuel was not afraid of the disease himself, which he said in a letter to John, he thought was caused by the general filthy conditions that prevail. *"I have no fear of it because I take my own proper measures to keep clean and healthy,"* he wrote. It is clear that Samuel thought the epidemic danger greatly exaggerated and went on to say, *"When one case of cholera appears, everyone who has a bellyache imagines he is stricken."*

The truth of his words was proved to him on the steamer, a few of the passengers complained of feeling unwell and before long, half of those on board were describing symptoms, either real or imagined. The cry went out for a doctor but there was none on board, those that there were having elected to stay behind and treat the sick. Panic was setting in and somebody suddenly remembered that there was a doctor on board, the eminent Dr. Coult of London, Calcutta and New York!

In vain, Samuel protested that Dr. Coult was a doctor of science not medicine but the frightened passengers were in no mood to split hairs, a doctor was a doctor after all, they wanted treatment and treatment they would have.

Samuel's reluctance to pose as a healer was interpreted as his holding out for an exorbitant fee and he realised that he would either have to adopt the role of healer or risk being thrown overboard.

He chose the former and after obtaining a supply of potent purgatives from the steamboats limited supplies, he set up his apparatus and both administered the purgative and administered the nitrous oxide gas, after all he reasoned, even if he did them no good, he would do them no harm and it was better to take that risk rather than a ducking in the river.

He had shrewdly suspected that there was not much wrong with his patients, except too much rich food, and after him ministrations, nature was quick to cooperate. Within forty-eight hours all symptoms of illness had vanished and Dr. Coult was hailed as the greatest healer of all time.

Samuel's conscience prevented him from taking a doctor's fee and also saw him decline to accept the purse that had been collected among his fellow passengers. Those who felt Dr. Coult had saved their lives, however, felt duty bound to spread the word of his good works, the news of which travelled along the river faster than the boat. Samuel had to go into hiding as he was besieged by would be patients at every landing.

A letter he wrote home to Hartford indicated his incredulity, *"If people are cheated, they cannot blame the cheater if they demand to be fooled as they have done with me."* So reluctant was he to take money from those demanding that he heal them, that he often gave medicine free, leaving him out of pocket.

He stopped in Cincinnati to allow his fame as a medicine man to subside and to discuss his future plans with John. In talking to John, he was shocked to discover that his brother had no objection to taking money from people under false pretences and thought that Samuel has missed a great opportunity to fill his coffers.

He suggested that it was not too late to cash in on Samuel's reputation as a healer and that if Samuel's conscience prevented him from charging a fee, then he could instead accept contributions. It was possible they could make more like that anyway. John would take over managing the tour and Samuel would be asked to prescribe only to those who insisted on seeing him.

John, it turned out, had built up debts and his creditors were threatening him with jail. Samuel made arrangements with John's creditors that kept him out of jail but it meant that Samuel had to give them over half of the takings from his river boat tour. Then, with people still calling at John's door demanding to see Dr. Coult, Samuel left Cincinnati and once again set out on the road as a wandering showman.

Eventually he reached Baltimore where he redeemed the first working model of his gun. It was a small calibre but well made and functioned so well that he decided to have a line of samples made in various calibres and even extended his idea to a rifle.

Through a man named, A. W. Baxter, Samuel arranged to hire a John Pearson to do the work. Samuel was to provide the money for materials, shop rent, and Pearson's wages as the labour progressed. Wanting to stay close to where the work was being done, Samuel took an engagement at the Baltimore Museum under the management of Joseph E. Walker. The venture at the museum was not a success and Samuel persuaded Baxter to endorse a $200 note. Paying Pearson a few weeks wages in advance and promising to send Baxter weekly amounts to take care of the note, Dr. Coult set off for Montreal to carry the story of nitrous oxide to the Canadians.

Samuel's first two bookings in Montreal were disappointing to say the least, the lecture halls being only half full. It took him a few days to realise that half the population spoke and read in French. He sought advice and was told that his advertising should be in French and that his lecture should also be in that language. He was also advised that if he wanted full houses, then he would need to take his show to Quebec, obtain good reports in the French papers and then return to Montreal.

Samuel also learned that patents were issued by the colonial governor and council in Quebec and not at the British patent office in London as he had supposed.

He needed no further incentive to go to Quebec, he would apply for his Canadian patents, replenish his purse and arrange for the press notices that would attract full houses on his return to Montreal. Samuel also employed a young Frenchman to accompany him to Quebec, to act as interpreter and to teach him to give his lecture in French.

Disaster! When they arrived in Quebec it was in the grip of yet another cholera scare. After his experiences on the Mississippi, Samuel did think that maybe he could help out, knowing that a lot of those who thought themselves sick were in fact just scared, but some people had died and in a letter to John he wrote, "*I thought I might be of some help as I had been on the river, but there have been a number of deaths and I could not risk making a mistake between the sick and those only thinking themselves to be so. I cannot do any business here for the present.*"

A fee of one hundred dollars was required on his application for patents on his revolver and by this time his funds were running low, he was worried that he might become stranded in Canada. He wrote to Walker explaining his predicament and suggesting a loan but Walker was also low on funds and could send him nothing but good wishes.

Samuel did not want to leave Canada without his patents, so he took advantage of the chorea scare to rent a theatre under a percentage agreement that enabled him to give four performances to virtually empty houses without cost to himself, beyond a small outlay for advertising. The newspaper editors, having been told this time what Samuel wanted, were generous in their notices, thus giving him the material he needed to attract customers on his return to Montreal.

Samuel received a letter from Baxter in Baltimore reminding him that the weekly remittances to cover his note were due but had not been forthcoming. Baxter knew of the situation in Quebec and was a little sympathetic but said that he had to have something with which to pay Pearson, who had nothing to live on but his wages.

Samuel did not immediately reply, indeed, he waited until he had received a further two letters. Samuel then wrote to Walker, asking that he try to pacify Baxter and Pearson for a while as Samuel had business he could do in Canada.

Walker accomplished his mission but warned Samuel that he could not keep Baxter quiet and Pearson at work indefinitely by powers of persuasion alone.

It was not until July 1834, three months after receiving Baxter's first letter, that Samuel was able to spare any funds and he sent fifty dollars to Walker, explaining that he should divide the money up in whatever way would do the most good.

He would remain in Montreal until August and would then proceed to Halifax and St. John.

On September 30th 1834, Samuel wrote to Walker again, this time with a long list of instructions but he sent no money. Walker replied, saying that Pearson had quit and would do no more work until paid, but it would appear that Samuel did not believe that Pearson had quit.

When he had been in Quebec, Samuel had learned that a great deal of money was to be made smuggling cloth across the border into America. At the time Samuel had been advised against any such enterprise by his father, explaining that the dangers were too great. Now however, in a letter back to Walker, Samuel repeated his list of instructions and then went on to say that soon, everyone would be paid in full, as he had invested all his spare funds in broadcloth on which he expected a very large profit, as he hoped to bring it in free of duty. Walker would hear from him when he reached Newport, he would dispose of his broadcloth there and settle his accounts.

It would appear, however, that things did not work out as Samuel had wished and, in a letter, dated November 2nd 1834 he writes, *"Since my last I have been lecturing in this place, and out of my receipts I have taken twenty-five dollars which is all I can spare at this time. It is a little better than nothing. I mentioned in my last that I had bought a couple of pieces of superfine broadcloths. One of them I got on shore free of duty, but the other, unfortunately, fell into the hands of the custom house officers owing to the carelessness of the captain and to recover which, I would have to pay near its value and not having the money at hand will probably lose it. If so, I shan't lose much more than the original cost, as the piece I have will bring nearly what the both cost. I shall not sell it if I can get along without it, until I get where the market is better than this place. In consequence of this, I have made up my mind to spend a couple of weeks in Massachusetts in hopes of making it good. I start from here tomorrow for Boston. I did well there in 1832 and as next is election and Thanksgiving week, I presume my receipts will be large. Whether they are or not I shall be supplied with money for the future. Write me how Pearson is getting along with his work. What are your prospects? I was not able to obtain all United States money. Consequently, one of the enclosed notes is of New York. I presume it is at par in Baltimore."*

When Samuel first started out in his role as a showman, he had heeded his father's advice about not spending money until he had it but after spending time with his brother John and Walker, he seems to have abandoned the practice and is much more nonchalant about having creditors.

Samuel did well in Boston and forwarded one hundred dollars to Walker with instructions to divide it between Pearson and Baxter.

Walker replied on 28th December, saying that he had found it necessary to divert the money to his own personal use. The money would neither pay Pearson nor satisfy Baxter so Walker had borrowed it in order to get to Richmond. He had left Baltimore in haste and at night to avoid being arrested for debt. There would have been no advantage in paying any money to Pearson because the man had quit working and would not resume until he had been paid his arrears and received a substantial advance on any future wages.

Walker suggested that Samuel come to Richmond where he had secured a job as manager of a theatre and predicted a long and successful run. The gate receipts would be divided half and half and Samuel would be charged five dollars a day for advertising and incidental expenses.

Samuel decided to accept Walker's proposal and joined him in Richmond, where his shows were a great success. As soon as receipts started to come in Samuel wrote to Pearson, urging him not to take employment from any other and that he would go to Baltimore to settle his account and he sent Pearson fifty dollars on account. He ordered Pearson to purchase tools and materials and to start work forthwith, saying that his wages would be nine dollars a week for a ten-hour six-day week, or ten dollars for a week of six twelve-hour days.

Pearson resented the tone of Samuel's letter and demanded nine dollars a week until April 1st and ten dollars a week thereafter for a ten-hour six-day week, he added, *"And for your offer of ten dollars a week for twelve hours, I take it to be an insult, one extra day for a dollar, I'd spend it on candles. The fifty dollars will not pay all your bill and you order me to buy a lot of things and then wait six months or your pleasure for my money. No baby bargain. Pay me my money due. Advance money for materials, and a month's wages in advance. So, you can use your own pleasure whether you employ me or not."*

A somewhat frustrated Samuel sent Pearson seventy-five dollars and repeated his instructions to start work, pointing out that the sooner Pearson started turning out revolvers the sooner he would be in a position to pay him better and regular wages.

Pearson, still not happy with the way he had been treated, nevertheless resumed work and on February 10th 1835 he wrote and told Samuel that he had hired space in a shop from one, Eratt.

Further disappointment was to follow. Samuel heard that the state of Virginia was about to purchase rifles for its militia and he knew and was in close touch with politicians who could *"Swing the order his way."* Samuel asked Pearson to forward the weapons as quickly as possible but Pearson had no rifle barrels. It also transpired that Samuel had overestimated the influence of the politicians and when he approached the Militia officers, he was told that they had a low opinion of Walker and his associates and would in any case not do business with a showman who owed everyone that would advance him credit. As for Samuel himself, they would not consider entrusting the arming of their troops to the proprietor of a one-man shop.

It was time for him to leave Richmond and make his way to Lynchburg and once he had set up headquarters there, he sent Pearson fifty dollars on March 25th 1835 with a letter advising him to start work with the upmost diligence.

On April 5th Colt received a reply from Walker, who was on the move again, a fugitive from Richmond for debt. Walker said he needed a loan of twenty or thirty dollars or he would be *"utterly ruined."*

Samuel sent Walker the requested twenty dollars and then, on hearing from Pearson that several guns were ready, he cancelled his remaining lecture engagements and set out for Baltimore.

Having settled with Pearson for the work completed he made new arrangements with him, increasing his wages to twelve dollars and fifty cents a week and promoting him to the position of foreman and hiring one Fred H. Brash as help at seven dollars and fifty cents a week.

Leaving Pearson two months pay for himself and Brash, Samuel set out for Hartford to seek financial backing. Samuel Colts life as Dr. Coult was now behind him.

Chapter Five

Paterson company formed

Samuel put his father Christopher in charge of finances and once again his father urged caution and advised against expanding too quickly, his own early experiences fresh in his mind.

He urged that Samuel be content to start out in business in a small way and to expand gradually as orders came in. He was afraid that if they raised money by selling stock, or worse still borrowed, and orders were slow, then they could be out of business and ruined very quickly.

Samuel howeer, dismissed his father's plea for caution. President Jackson had forced the French to pay five million dollars in compensation for American property damaged in the Napoleonic wars and the government was certain to spent a portion of that money on the army and navy.

Armed conflict looked a real possibility and if they could get into a position to handle federal orders Colt felt that he could have a virtual monopoly on military business.

Christopher most have caught some of his son's enthusiasm, he thought that once he had established his corporation he would have little difficulty in selling shares but before this could be done, he would have to secure patents both in the United States and abroad. He already had some protection, because of the description of his gun that he had filed in Washington when he was on his lecture tour, what he needed now was foreign patents.

In the end Samuel and Christopher turned to Aunt Ethalinda Selden in Troy, New York. Ethalinda sent her husband Joseph to Hartford with one thousand dollars. For that sum Joseph was assigned a one quarter share in Colt's patents, Christopher also received a quarter share in his son's patents.

In August 1835 Colt left for England and France to secure his foreign patents. In a letter to his father Samuel complained of the slowness of the process but although the delay was putting considerable strain on his purse, Samuel did not think it wise to appear impatient.

He was also disappointed with the attitude of the British towards his invention, an attitude that was supported by the likes of celebrated sportsman and author, Colonel Peter Hawker, who had once written of the introduction of the percussion cap, "*When flintlock guns were the order of the day, few sporting gentlemen of distinction ever thought of using anything but the gun of a first-rate maker, for the simple reason that, on the goodness of the work depended the quickness of firing, and consequently, the filling of the bag. But now-a-days, every common fellow in a market town can detonate an old musket and make it shoot as quick as can be wished; insomuch that all scientific calculations in shooting, at moderate distances, are now so simplified, that we every day meet with jackanape-apprentice-boys who can shoot birds flying and knock down their eight out of ten."*

With such attitudes towards the percussion cap, one can imagine what their attitude would be towards a repeating arm.

Officials at the British patent office tried in vain to find a valid reason to deny Colt his patent but could find none, so despite their reluctance to grant a patent to an alien, Samuel Colt was awarded his patent.

From London, Samuel travelled to the continent and obtained some rights in France and Prussia but he was forced to abandon his planned trip to Russia because of lack of funds.

Returning home, he reached Hartford in January 1836 and finding his father in funds, he borrowed an additional eight hundred dollars, went to Washington and obtained his patents in February 1836.

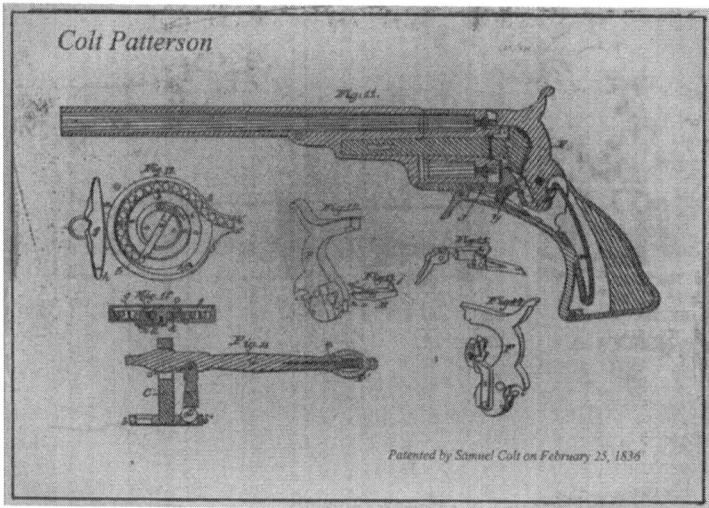

Colt's patent

With his patents safely in hand and a loan from his cousin Dudley Selden, together with letters of recommendation from Henry Ellsworth, Colt formed a corporation of venture capitalists. With the help of these venture capitalists and their political friends, The Patent Arms Manufacturing Company of Paterson, New Jersey, was chartered by the New Jersey legislature on 5th March 1836.

Thomas Addis Emmet, Elias B. D. Ogden, Daniel K. Allen, Daniel Holsman and Elias Vanarsdale were elected board of directors and a disused silk mill in Paterson was leased as a factory.

Colt was given a remuneration for each gun sold in exchange for his patent rights, and it was agreed that should the company stop manufacture for any reason, all rights would return to Samuel. Samuel was to receive a salary of one thousand dollars a year and the right in the first year to purchase fifty thousand dollar's worth of stock. In return, he was to devote not more than nine months getting the factory up and running and giving such aid to business as might be needed.

Samuel manoeuvered to have his cousin, Dudley Selden, the son of Aunt Ethalinda and Uncle Joseph made secretary of the company with the job of general manager as well, a decision that he would later regret. Dudley was a lawyer, accountant, and banker who was meticulously ethical in his business transactions and an ideal watchdog for the Colt family interests.

Whilst all this activity was taking place, Samuel's remittances to Pearson in Baltimore had been few and far between but he now wrote to the mechanic and ordered him to forward all the guns he had.

Pearson replied that the last money he had been sent was long spent and that he had pledged his personal credit to keep the shop going. He had now been compelled to stop working and was in danger of being jailed for debt contracted in Colt's business. He begged Samuel to send a substantial sum.

Samuel showed no empathy towards the man and replied, *"What do you mean by disappointing me in this fashion?"*

In his reply, Pearson pointed out all the difficulties he'd had collecting money from Samuel and wrote, *"You make nothing of disappointing me, but you do not like I should disappoint you."* He wanted fifty dollars without delay, and when he had the money, he would consider turning over such arms as were finished.

In order to pay Pearson, Samuel needed orders for guns but he could not secure them without samples, everything depended on getting the guns. In the end Samuel borrowed the money from Dudley and paid.

Dudley had opened a New York office for the company at, 69 Cedar Street and had set about collecting the money for the stock subscriptions.

The subscribers, however, were loath to part with cash and instead offered their notes which, they pointed out, could be discounted at any bank without difficulty. Dudley however, insisted that the company should have two hundred and thirty thousand dollars in actual cash and not that amount or any fraction of it, in potential obligations. The stock subscribers shrugged their shoulders and said he could either take their notes or cancel the subscriptions.

Samuel urged Dudley to accept the notes, *"Let's get to making the arms of my invention without delay,"* he pleaded in a letter from the factory in Paterson to Dudley in New York. Samuel even travelled to New York to put his case to Dudley, only to have Dudley point out that Samuel's role was to get the factory set up and running and that the financing of the business was none of his concern.

Samuel returned to Paterson regretting introducing cousin Dudley to the company. Once back, he offered the job of foreman to Pearson but Pearson demanded too many guarantees so Thomas Lawton, another Baltimore gunsmith, was given the job and Samuel began arranging the factory with an eye on quick quality production.

Samuel Colt had really always had two visions, the first was to produce a reliable gun that would have a cylinder rotated automatically as the gun was cocked and then locked in position for firing, the second was to manufacture his guns in such a way that they would have interchangeable parts. His idea was to have the parts made by machine and assembled by hand on something resembling a modern assembly line.

His idea had been made clear in a letter he wrote to his father in 1836 in which he wrote, "*The first workman would receive two or three of the most important parts and would affix these and pass them on to the next who would add a part and pass the growing article on to another who would do the same, and so on until the completed arm is put together.*"

He knew that Eli Whitney had made some parts of government muskets by machinery and that the United States Armoury at Springfield, Massachusetts, had machines for certain operations, so he saw no reason why every operation in the manufacture of his own guns couldn't be done in that way.

Chapter Six

Family strife

When Dudley learned that Samuel was experimenting with mass production machinery, he lost no time in informing him that the company funds were to be used for manufacturing guns and not for experimenting with new-fangled contraptions with which to turn then out. He ordered Samuel to stop his tinkering and to purchase standard shop equipment, set it up and start producing guns.

Samuel argued that his patent revolvers would be too expensive if produced by hand but Dudley would have none of it. He ruled that if merchants could not afford to carry stock then guns could be made to order, in the meantime the factory could earn dividends by making a line of inexpensive single shot firearms.

Sam refused to produce anything but his own arms and the factory began producing revolvers on a small scale but it wasn't long before Seldon was complaining that orders were not coming in as Samuel had predicted. Samuel repeated his argument that the guns were too dear and pleaded that he be allowed to develop the machinery to be able to make them cheaply, but Dudley refused to allow any such expenditure.

Selden continued to complain about the lack of customers and hinted that perhaps Samuel's invention wasn't as good as he had claimed.

Samuel countered by enquiring what Selden was doing to create a market and it turned out that he was simply waiting for the public to ask for his product, what else could a respectable manufacturer do?

Sam demanded that he let the world know what he had to offer by advertising in newspapers, sending out salesmen and demonstrators and making gifts of revolvers to prominent people and persuading them to praise the arms.

Seldon was shocked that Samuel should believe him capable of consenting to any such methods of promoting business. Did Samuel have no pride? Did he expect to conduct the affairs of a great corporation in the manner of a street corner medicine show? Such practises, he declared, were beneath the dignity of a Selden.

Well such practises were not beneath the dignity of Samuel Colt. He set out from Paterson on a selling tour, giving demonstrations and lectures in general stores in an effort to get merchants to purchase at least one sample of his revolver. He had some success but the royalties he received did not cover his expenses and he was soon out of funds.

He once again turned to his father for a loan, but Christopher thought his son was overwrought and his stepmother Olive suggested he come home at Thanksgiving for a rest, but it wasn't a rest Samuel needed, it was sales.

Instead, Samuel obtained a small loan from his cousin, Roswell Colt and went to Washington where he showed his invention to President Jackson. The President was impressed but was leaving office in a few months and did not want to leave his successor with a problem involving the rearming of the military. He assured Samuel that the incoming Mr Van Buren could be depended on to do something about it. The President accepted a finely engraved revolver as a sample of Colt's invention and having tested it, sent Samuel a note commending him for having made a substantial improvement in firearms.

With this note and Jackson's approval Samuel managed to get a bill through Congress authorising an official test of his revolver by an army board. The bill however carried no appropriation and the War Department declined to do any testing until specifically dedicated funds were made available for the purpose.

Samuel looked then to South Carolina, where the Militia were looking to buy arms and were interested in the revolver in both pistol and rifle models but they wanted guarantees of prompt delivery. They were intent on building up a militia superior to that of the federal government. They did not trust Van Buren, a New Yorker and therefore tainted with the anti-slavery notions of John Quincy Adams and the high tariff principles favoured by northern industrialists.

Samuel wrote urging that the factory be speeded up to capacity and asking how many arms could be sent. He was informed that seventy-five pistols could be with him in three weeks but that rifles would not be available for at least two months. A further blow to Samuel's hopes came when he heard that Selden would not permit the shop to make them until they were ordered and paid for.

Sam tried his best to convey the urgency of the situation, pointing out that Eli Whitney's armoury was ready to deliver several hundred muskets within a week and that Whitney's arm, although inferior to Colt's, was much cheaper but that the Carolinians were willing to pay the higher price if they could get the guns right away. Samuel stressed that speed of delivery was the key to obtaining the contract.

Selden was uncertain and by the time he finally yielded to Samuel's demands the contract had been awarded to Whitney.

Samuel's note informing the Paterson office of the loss of the South Carolina contract was sent just before the arrival of one hundred revolvers with a letter from Selden instructing

Samuel to collect the payment for them at once and send the money promptly, the word promptly was underlined.

Samuel canvassed the militia officers and managed to sell about seventy-five revolvers, but he did not send the money immediately and when called to account by Selden, Samuel's reply laid the blame for the loss of the contract squarely at Selden's feet. Nobody but himself, he complained, was making any attempt to sell the guns and he was unable to obtain deliveries for the business he obtained.

He went on to request that he might make a small drawing on the account so that he could see what business could be done in Washington now that Mr. Van Buren was in office.

Possibly feeling that he was in some small part to blame for the loss of the contract, Selden agreed to the request. When Samuel arrived, he found the Capital a very different place from the one he had visited before, with much in-fighting in Congress. Samuel managed to take advantage of the situation and with much promising and entertaining, manoeuvered himself into a place of influence and succeeded in having money appropriated for the test that had been authorised under Jackson.

Samuel knew that there were two schools of thought in the Ordnance Bureau, there were the old brass hats that thought the smooth bore musket and single shot pistol were the last word in military equipment and then there were the more progressive younger ranks that thought firearm improvement was well overdue. Samuel knew that he needed his gun tested by the latter, because if his gun received an adverse report, he would be in a worse position that if the tests hadn't taken place.

Samuel was prepared to persuade, bribe or even bully to get his way but in the end, Selden called a halt to Samuel's spending and when the testing board was appointed by the Ordnance Bureau, it included two brigadiers, a colonel, a lieutenant colonel, a major, a captain and a lieutenant.

The brigadiers and the colonels were advocates of the good old muskets and one suspects that the junior officers were too aware of their own interests to take issue with the mature judgment of their seniors.

Colt's gun was tested at West Point in June, along with several other arms. The board disapproved of all of them, but added about Colt's offering, "*that from its complicated character, its liability to accident and other reasons, this arm is entirely unsuited to the general purpose of the service*."

The report was a huge blow for Samuel but not entirely unexpected, he now desperately needed something that would soften the impact of the report on his commercial prospects.

His hopes were revived when he learned that the navy

wanted to test his revolver. In the past the navy had usually disagreed with the findings of the army, so Samuel was optimistic. His hopes, however, were dashed once again when the navy broke precedent and agreed with the army's assessment.

Samuel was depressed and discouraged for the first time in his life as he returned to Paterson and to rub salt into his wounds, no sooner had he arrived than, he was arrested on a warrant obtained by a creditor. Bail was set at $250 and it was only begrudgingly paid by the arms company. He was then summoned to a meeting of unhappy stockholders, who demanded that he either settle his accounts or surrender the rights to his patents.

Samuel was unable to raise the cash but was determined not to surrender the rights to his patents. He proposed that the company allow him to have one hundred guns on credit and pay him a commission on the sales, all of this money, except modest living expenses, would be returned to the company until the debt was paid and the company, despite Selden's reluctance, agreed.

Samuel first visited Florida, where there was conflict between federal troops and Seminole, a tribe of Native Americans. Second in command of operations against the Seminole was Colonel William S. Harney, an officer Samuel had met in Washington and one who had been impressed by Samuel's invention. His Commanding officer, one General Thomas S. Jessup, had authority to purchase whatever his troops needed and Samuel was confident he would purchase all of his guns if Harney recommended them.

Colonel William S. Harney
1800 - 1889

General Thomas S. Jessup
1788 – 1860
Jessup served in the
American army for 52 years

Samuel arrived in Fort Jupiter, East Florida, with his hundred guns but in spite of Harney's endorsement, Jessop declined to take the whole consignment and purchased only fifty rifles. He gave Samuel a draft for $6,250 on Lieutenant Clark, finance officer at Black Creek. Samuel also sold some twelve pistols to officers and so with the money from the sale of the pistols and Jessop's draft for the rifles, he struck out for St. Augustine.

Fate turned against him once again, as the boat taking him down the Indian River took seven days to reach St. Augustine and could not get into harbour. Several passengers, including the young Samuel, tried to make it ashore in a small boat, but the boat capsized and Samuel only narrowly escaped drowning. In his efforts to stay afloat until recued he lost Jessop's draft and when finally on dry land he had only the cash he had collected from the officers which he had kept separate.

On the 11th April 1838 Samuel wrote to Dudley, telling him of the unfortunate events, and to General Jessop to request a duplicate draft. The General declined Samuel's request, pointing out that the draft was as good as cash and if it should ever be presented, he would be responsible for honouring it. Samuel would need to get an act of Congress passed to pay him the money and relieve the General of the responsibility.

The next blow to be visited on Samuel, as if he needed one, came with cousin Dudley's reply. He could not understand how anyone could lose $6250, capsized boat or no capsized boat. The tone of the letter implied that Dudley had doubts about the truth of Samuel's account of events. In any case, a contract is a contract and he pointed out that Samuel had agreed to send the money as soon as the guns were sold, so

Samuel would have to find the money from somewhere and settle his account. Dudley said that he didn't *"wish to be harsh"* so he would wait a reasonable time before taking legal action.

That Uncle Joseph Seldon had died in the autumn of 1837, Samuel knew. Although unable to attend the funeral in person, he had sent his condolences and arranged for flowers to be delivered.

What Samuel was unaware of at that time, was that part of cousin Dudley's inheritance was the stock that Uncle Joseph had purchased in the arms company as well as the $1,000 note that had financed Samuel's patent seeking trip to Europe. This made Dudley, not just an agent of the company, but a substantial stock holder.

Samuel ignored Dudley's demands and travelled north west to Charleston, where he managed to sell another dozen pistols. He wrote to Dudley to tell him of the sale and in reply Dudley once again demanded cash for all the arms sold and the return of those as yet unsold.

An angry and frustrated Samuel returned to Paterson and told Dudley exactly what he thought of him and stated that from that time on he would leave the selling of arms to Dudley, he would simply collect his royalties on the sale and take no further part.

As for the debts, the company could get that by selling guns and retaining Samuel's royalties until it was paid off. If the company ceased to manufacture and sell the guns, Samuel would withdraw from the company the right to manufacture and they could sue for the money. He was tired of being handicapped in all he tried to do by a penny-pinching policy that he argued was killing his invention.

After leaving Dudley's office in a rage, Samuel contacted Richard Pullen, an Englishman who had once considered helping Samuel establish an English factory. A Contract was signed giving Pullen an interest in the profits of the company and Samuel was guaranteed capital of up to ten thousand pounds, five hundred of which was paid up front.

Dudley, on hearing that Samuel had come into funds, demanded that the money be turned over to him and said that if Samuel tried to sail without paying, he would be arrested at the docks.

Samuel pointed out that he now had a guarantee of some capital and that it would be in everyone's best interest to let him go to England and establish himself.

Dudley was all set to let Samuel go, when he was dealt yet another blow and Pullen informed Samuel that he had been unable to raise the money. In pure frustration, Samuel took a leaf out of Dudley's book and informed Pullen that a contract is a contract and that either the money promised must be raised or Samuel would keep the five hundred pounds as a forfeit.

Pullen sued for the return of the five hundred pounds but lost the case. However, from that time on, Samuel was to be engaged in some form of litigation almost every year for the rest of his life.

Out of the money from Pullen he repaid some of his debt and Dudley allowed him to be an agent for the company's products with a line of credit and in response Samuel applied himself to getting Congress to authorise payment of the lost Jessop draft, which they did.

He received the draft for $6,250 dated 21st June 1838 and when Dudley began to press him on the matter, he handed over, not just the draft but also a letter from Lieutenant Clark, stating, for the benefit of "*all who might be concerned*," that the Jessop draft had never been cashed with Clark, effectively proving that Samuel's account of the loss of the draft had been entirely truthful. This at least partially settled Samuel's accounts with Seldon and the company.

Samuel was now attempting to sell his arms to the commercial trade rather than government, and had several thousand dollars worth out on consignment. When he wrote to Dudley suggesting that a certain party might be helpful if given a substantial gift, Dudley was shocked by the suggestion and wrote that the suggestion was, *"the most dishonourable he ever had heard and he would not tolerate any such action."*

He then demanded that the arms he had sent Samuel be returned to the factory, if Samuel could not sell them then the factory could use them to fill orders.

Samuel informed Dudley that he had been forced to pledge some of the arms as security for loans to pay his expenses, and in his reply dated 24th February 1839 Dudley wrote, *"Your letter of the 21st is before me and I assure you I have read it with surprise and regret. By what authority have you placed the property of the Patent Arms Company in the hands of anyone and thereupon drawn funds for your private expenditures? And, it seems that, independent of sales, the property of the company is to remain as security for your debts to your banker.*

"I know not what you may think of the morels of this business, but it seems to me not much better than putting your hand in a man's pocket. I write this at my house and state generally that some of the goods have been received back from you at the store, but whether the articles correspond with those mentioned in your letter I cannot state, and let me further say that if the residue is not immediately accounted for, greater difficulties may arise than you anticipate.

"Heretofore I supposed that the only ground of

complaint relative to the goods received by you for sale, except as to what you sold in New York, was that you had wholly abandoned every effort to sell them, but it now turns out that you have been living on the proceeds of those sold and intend to leave other portions of them as security to your banker. This matter will be laid before the directors forthwith as a meeting has been called for Thursday by the president on important business and you may as well understand distinctly that I will not remain a single day in the condition in which I am placed by your unfair course after you have received this letter and have had sufficient time to answer it.

"Before the present week is out, I will take the necessary steps to indemnify myself, so far as the security placed in my hands will enable me to do it. As to its value, I have no faith in it. Years will go by, I fear, before it will make any adequate returns to a purchaser, if ever. All your promises have proved illusory. You wanted a sample carbine. It was sent to you under the express condition to be speedily returned to be sent to Albany. Mr. Zabriskie has now been detained here twenty days and it has not come and you now write about taking it to Richmond. You wanted some sample cones and a new formed cap primer to negotiate with the government. They were furnished and not a word is afterwards heard on the subject.

"You took goods to sell for the company at Harrisburg and Washington. You never went to Harrisburg and applied the proceeds of sales, which belonged to the company and put the goods in pledge to pay your own banker and expenses. You stated a long time ago that your delay in assigning the patent to the company was n order to make some necessary and useful changes by obtaining new patents at the patent office. At the end of sixty days there is no evidence to lay before the company that you have done anything.

"With respect to going to Richmond or not I have no advice to give. You have control over your own movements. I would barley remark that your efforts at Washington give me no confidence in what you may undertake to do elsewhere.

"I advise you to account and settle with the company for the property received from them without delay, and before you go anywhere except to New York. You may thereby be more certain master of your own time and movements than you are at present or may be after the meeting of directors."

Dudley's complaint about the position in which he had been placed referred to the fact that, as Samuel's cousin, he regarded himself as morally responsible for Samuel's conduct while selling on consignment. He had therefore insisted that Samuel post security with him before receiving guns from the company. The only asset he possessed was a patent on the waterproof cable, with some modifications, that he had used to blow up the raft on Ware Pond. His promise to turn over his patents to the company had only been made because of Dudley's threats after the loss of the Jessop draft and before he received the five hundred pounds from Pullen. It is doubtful that Samuel would ever have actually relinquished ownership of his revolver patents.

In answering Dudley's letter Samuel simply stated that he had now perfected a waterproof cartridge for his revolver and that he would send back such arms as he could spare. He had *"made engagements with some officers, members of congress and the secretary of war, which I am in honour bound to keep."*

Dudley was troubled by a report from, Zabriskie, a salesman who said that a pistol was missing from a consignment forwarded to him by Samuel. Was Samuel trying to force Dudley into taking drastic action? In fact, Samuel was actually using the pistol to convince a joint army and navy board of the virtues of his invention, but he suspended his meeting with the board to travel to Paterson for a showdown.

Samuel told the directors bluntly that it was useless trying to gain a government contract without spending money. Yes, he had pledged some of the guns sent to him in order to get the funds needed to live while fighting to gain business.

Dudley had refused to advance him any cash. How did they expect him to support himself while promoting the interests of the company and stockholders?

Fortunately for Samuel, the directors saw his point about supporting himself but could not agree on any plan to finance his trip to Washington and it was too late anyway. Dudley's actions meant that it would be at least another six months before another meeting could be scheduled.

Some directors argued that it was up to Colt to market his invention and that the company was only obliged to finance its production. If Colt lacked the means to pay his own expenses then he should surrender his patents, waive his royalties and work for the company for a salary, a point of view which Dudley enthusiastically supported, after all, he pointed out, Samuel was still only twenty-four, his activities needed to be supervised and controlled.

Thomas Addis Emmet disagreed, he had faith in Colt's invention and a better understanding of long-term goals than Dudley, who could only think in terms of immediate returns.

Emmet's inability to convince his fellow directors cost him and ultimately the company dear, as he observed years later when he wrote to acknowledge a gift from Colt in a letter dated May 28th 1852.

"My dear Sir.

The pistol which you forwarded me by express came to hand yesterday. I thank you for your kindness in remembering me and I accept it in the spirit with which it has been sent, as an offering to "auld lang syne," and as such it shall never be parted with.

"It did not, however, require such a splendid specimen of your revolver to remind me frequently of you. I confess that a more sordid feeling, to wit, the conviction of how much I and those associated with us in the Patent Arms Company have lost in a pecuniary point of view, often revolves in my mind. I was always a firm believer in the utility and ultimate success of your arms, and used all my endeavours to adjust the unfortunate disagreements which served us asunder, but it was of no avail, and while I regret my own loss, I most sincerely wish that you may reap the full and rich reward which so valuable an invention deserves, and long to enjoy it."

Another director, Daniel K. Allen, doubted that Samuel would ever accept a salaried position and give up his patents and he had heard there was a chance that the militia of the state of Maine might be of a mind to buy some of Colt's guns and suggested that Samuel should be sent there. He reasoned also that it would give Colt time to make up his mind concerning the Board's proposal.

Samuel rejected any suggestion that he should accept a salary and as for going to Maine, if that was what the company wanted then he would go, but he pointed out that the real place to sell his arms was in Washington. Once the national forces adopted the weapon the militia of the states would follow.

He requested the company extend his credit by an additional $600 in addition to the $900 he already owed. He would take a supply of arms with him because he didn't want to find himself in the position where he had sold guns the factory was unable to deliver.

The directors accepted Samuel's proposal, much to Dudley's dismay. Emmet and Allen explained to Samuel that he need no longer worry about the threats of legal action against him for pledging the company's property, but they warned him against making such mistakes in the future.

When Samuel arrived in Maine, the legislature had adjourned and nothing could be done until the next session.

The fifty dollars the company had advanced him barely covered the cost of the trip and he was low on funds again. Samuel received several offers of financial help from businessmen who were impressed with his gun, but with

Emmet's and Allen's advice in mind he declined to pledge the company's property.

Instead he wrote to Paterson of his plight and it would appear that Dudley, who had been expecting the worst, was so impressed by Samuel's refusal to pledge the company's property, that he sent twenty-five dollars for his passage back to New York and arranged for the return of the guns. Dudley was so pleased with Samuel's behaviour and possibly a little embarrassed at having sent him to Maine without determining whether the legislator was sitting, that when Samuel proposed that he resume his activity in Washington, Dudley raised no objection.

Whilst travelling to and from Portland, Maine, Samuel had perfected the design of his waterproof cartridge. The cartridge held the powder in a tinfoil cylinder with the bullet attached and the joints sealed with wax.

The cartridge was an important step forward in firearm development, a point that was entirely missed by Dudley and the other directors.

In Washington, Colonel Buford dismissed Samuel's model for a waterproof cartridge as being too small at .34 calibre. The Colonel held that nothing short of a one-once ball was of any use for military purposes. Samuel argued in vain that a six-shooter of such a calibre would be too cumbersome to use and that he would demonstrate on any animal up to and including a buffalo that .34 calibre was enough. Joel E. Poinsett, the Secretary for War, considered that Samuel's point was probably sound but he declined to overrule the Colonel.

As Samuel was about to leave Washington, he encountered a delegation of frontiersmen from the new Republic of Texas who were there to urge upon Congress, its admission as a state in the Union.

Samuel discovered from them that they were familiar with his gun and rated it highly. Captain Sam H. Walker of the Texas Rangers, was in New York to purchase guns at a reduced price from dealers who were tired of having unsold revolvers in stock. The factory price was too high they claimed, but they had found that some dealers were willing to get rid of unsold stock at a loss.

Samuel made a bee line for New York and on not finding Walker at his lodgings in the Aster House, made a tour of the local stores and eventually caught up with him in the shop of Samuel Hall.

Hall was only too willing to part with his stock as they had proved impossible to sell after the unfavourable report of the army and navy had been published.

Walker paid no mind to the army and navy reports; he had used the revolver in actual combat and knew it to be the best arm so far developed. He had been one of fifteen Texas Rangers with Captain John Coffee Hays when, armed with Colt's revolvers, they had defeated seventy-five Comanches, killing over thirty of them.

John Coffee Hayes, known as Jack Hayes or Captain Jack, was a tough frontiersman from Tennessee and had been appointed captain in the Texas Rangers in 1840. He had a fierce reputation, earned fighting both Indians and Mexican bandits. Hayes had been the first Ranger to come across Colt's revolver and had been so impressed with it he had armed his entire company with Colt's gun.

The Comanche were in the habit of coming out on top in encounters with Rangers. Their tactics were simple, they would almost always outnumber the Rangers anyway and would simply dodge as best they could when the Rangers fired on them, and then counter attack as the hapless Rangers were reloading, it worked every time.

This encounter had been very different, as the Rangers were able to keep firing as the Comanche attacked, mowing them down. Those Comanche who survived reported to their chief that; The Rangers had a shot for every finger on the hand!

Samuel introduced himself to Walker, expecting nothing but praise but Walker disappointed him. Yes, Walker said, you have invented a far superior arm, but why didn't you make a better job of it?

Captain John Coffee Hayes
Captain in the Texas Rangers who fought in several campaigns against the Comanche people and in the Mexican – American War.

Walker had used the arm in battle so Samuel was willing to listen to his criticism, and it was out of that meeting that the Walker-Colt, a much sturdier arm, was developed.

Samuel persuaded Dudley to have one hundred of them made up and sold to Walker at cost price, expecting the entire population of Texas to purchase one. What Samuel didn't take into account was that, with the hundred produced by the factory and the guns Walker had already managed to obtain cheaply from dealers, almost everybody in the sparsely populated state who had the price of one would be supplied by Walker.

Dudley predicted as much and wrote, "*It is poor business to sell your product without making a profit. If the purchaser wants it he will pay you a fair price. If he does not want it and there is demand for it sooner or later someone will pay you enough so that you can make a profit. You seem to think that this sale will mean that we shall not be able to keep up with the orders. This I do not believe. If there are those with large means in Texas who value your guns as highly as you appear to believe, in all likelihood the persons for whose account they are now purchased will dispose of them at a good profit to themselves, while the company makes no profit at all. However, I will not place myself in the position of appearing to interfere with what you seem to regard as a good stroke of business for the company, and I will supply the arms under the conditions you desire.*"

As it turned out, Dudley was right and the company only ever received a small number of orders from Texas.

Dudley had lost patiences with Samuel and withdrew his privilege of being able to draw money, ordered him to settle his affairs with the company and announced that until the stock of arms at the factory had been sold, no more would be made up. Instead, the factory would turn out a line of high-grade shotguns for which there appeared to be a demand, and Samuel could sell those.

His commission on the sale of shotguns was hardly enough to keep him fed and Samuel once again found himself in a financial crisis. His clothes were looking shabby and he wrote to his stepmother to send him some new. By the time they arrived he was so short of funds that he was unable to send her the fourteen dollars they had cost.

He once again reviewed the shotgun option but it would provide no more than a hand to mouth existence, so he consulted his friends Allen and Emmet. They persuaded the directors to allow stockholders to buy shotguns at cost. Dudley did not think many would take up the option but thought that it might stir up interest in the business among the stockholders and possibly even make some pay the balance of their stock subscriptions that were still owing.

He was however, surprised by the sudden demand for shotguns from the stockholders. That is, until he discovered to his horror that Samuel was selling the guns at just under the company's own price and using the proceeds to pay off all his debtors except Dudley and the arms company. It didn't take him long to realise why the stockholders were buying so many guns. He called a meeting of the directors and demanded that the privilege be withdrawn.

The directors refused. Dudley resigned and immediately filed suit against Samuel for $303.34 still due on the old note that Samuel had given to Uncle Joseph.

John Ehlers was elected to take Dudley's place and said that he would advance Samuel the funds he needed if he settled up the old account and assigned his patents to the company. If he did this the company would mark his debt paid and finance his marketing campaign. Otherwise Ehlers would be reluctantly forced to start a suit to collect.

Samuel agreed, but on the advice of Emmet and Allen, he stipulated that if the company ever suspended manufacture of his arms the patents should revert to him as provided in the original contract.

Ehlers did not object, he had no intention of stopping manufacture, he had great faith in Samuel's invention and believed that under his management a fortune could be made from it. However, it turns out, that he wanted the fortune for himself and had no intention of sharing it with Samuel or anyone else.

Chapter Seven

Submarine Mines

Encouraged by Ehlers attitude, Samuel went to Washington at the beginning of 1840 and stayed at Todd's Rooms, a popular lodging house.

An unexpected boom in cotton sales in the South helped to alleviate the depression that had followed Van Buren's inauguration. Most of the states were now pushing for federal government to spend money on roads, harbour improvements and buildings in order to create employment.

Samuel Colt, never slow to spot an opportunity, lost little time in proposing that the rearming of the army and navy would be another sensible use of federal funds and when Congress realised that the military appropriations bill proposed by Colt, could be made comprehensive enough to include almost anything they wanted, they readily approved it.

There now appeared on the scene one Mighill Nutting, a man who was trying to raise interest in a revolver he claimed to have invented, however, the design of Nutting's gun depended very much on Colt's basic patents. This shortcoming in Nutting's gun appears to have been overlooked by army and navy experts who declared the gun "practical" and advised Nutting to start production.

Nutting failed to attract investors however and eventually approached Samuel and offered him the chance to, *"buy out my interest in our conflicting patents."* Samuel examined Nutting's gun carefully and having determined that it could not be manufactured without infringing on his own patents, he declined the offer.

The military appropriations bill that Samuel had suggested fell through, as other political matters came to the forefront.

In 1837 the steamship Caroline had been carrying American recruits and munitions to rebels in Canada but while it was docked at the town of Schlosser on the American side, it had been stormed and taken by Canadian and British troops. During the attack, one American by the name of, Amos Durfee had been killed and the Caroline was set on fire and allowed to drift over the Niagara Falls. United States newspapers falsely reported "*the death of twenty-two of her crew*" when in fact, only Durfee was killed. President Martin Van Buren protested strongly to London, but his remonstrations were ignored.

In 1840, a Canadian sheriff named Alexander McLeod claimed that he had helped in the attack during the Caroline affair. McLeod was arrested in the United States in 1840 for his role in Durfee's death during the attack.

This caused yet another international incident, as the British demanded his release, stating that he should not be held criminally responsible for following orders. The trial attempted to identify who exactly had shot Durfee, but this proved futile. McLeod was then acquitted of all charges when witness statements made it clear that he he'd had no involvement in the Caroline incident at all. He had claimed to have been involved simply to gain some notoriety.

The trial not only stirred up anti British feeling in the United States, it caused a lot of people to ask, just where the recruits had obtained their arms? There was a great deal of publicity in the press denouncing gun dealers as war mongers and calls were made for tighter controls. In view of this display of public concern, it was decided not to anger voters by spending money on new arms for the army and navy.

The army and navy were not too bothered about not being rearmed with the new revolver, but the increased tension with Britain meant that they were concerned about protecting the country's harbours from British warships if hostilities should break out.

Congress was caught in a cleft stick, if they started building harbour defences the British might take it for war preparations and strike before they were completed and if they built them and no war came, voters would regard it as a waste of money.

Samuel was quick to explain to the War Department that he had a new invention, that of submarine mines that would protect any harbour from enemy attack. Once again Samuel's assertions fell on deaf ears, the only way to protect a harbour was to keep enemy shipping away from it by having a larger navy, he was told.

Samuel was not discouraged however, there had been one or two in the department that had listened and he was confident enough in their interest to form a new corporation. This time he would make sure that he retained control. He held the majority of the stock, issuing only small amounts to his father, his stepmother, his brothers James and John and his friends Emmet and Allen.

Sale of stock was easier than Samuel had anticipated. He gave no guarantees, he made it plain that if the government bought into his invention, there was a fortune to be made, but if not, they could not blame Samuel Colt, who had been completely honest and upfront about the prospects.

Stock sold well and for the first time in his life Samuel found himself with adequate funds. Realising that he could make no progress on his submarine mine until after the presidential elections, he gave up trying to push his own invention and instead, he obtained an order for several hundred standard muskets from the Bureau of Ordnance.

On arriving at the Paterson factory to inspect the work however, he was distressed to discover that Ehlers had been cutting costs and turning out an inferior musket. Samuel notified the Bureau of Ordnance at once and recommended that the order be cancelled, his advice was ignored however and the arms were delivered and accepted.

He also noticed that his shotgun sales were falling off although his customers were still carrying the Paterson made guns in stock. It turned out that Ehlers was selling the guns direct to the dealers at a price that undercut his own by precisely the amount of his commission.

Infuriated by being cheated in this way, Samuel wasted no time in filing suit against Ehlers and the arms company, demanding the right to inspect the books and damages of double the amount of his estimated loss due to Ehler's trickery.

He retained the firm of McCann and Clark who were experts in such matters and soon had Ehlers so tied up in litigation that the arms company, for all intents and purposes, was out of business.

Ehlers had no choice, other than to put the company into bankruptcy and manufacturing ceased. Samuel's lawyers found that Ehlers had taken Samuel's patents as security for a loan he had made to the company and immediately put a stop on him disposing of the patents or of making any use of them.

Eventually, under the terms of the clause that gave the patents back to Samuel if the company ever stopped manufacturing his guns, the patents were taken from Ehlers and returned to Samuel Colt.

And so, the first attempt to manufacture and sell the Colt revolver had ended in failure.

Samuel knew that the government of the United States was the only possible purchaser for his "submarine battery" as he called it, and because of that he had been paying more attention to the political arena. Samuel's submarine battery was basically an underwater minefield where the mines could be detonated electrically from a distance.

In Samuel's opinion, it seemed likely that Van Buren was going to be denied a second term, because as soon as he had taken office he had stopped behaving as a politician, and had ignored political expediency to do what would best serve the needs of the country without regard for his own political future.

All this he had done while those around him played politics to further their own interests. Samuel formed his own opinion of those who governed the country and it wasn't flattering. However, he believed he could handle such people and from what he had seen, he thought his chances of getting his invention adopted depended about ten per cent on its merits, twenty-five per cent on his own prominence and popularity and sixty-five per cent on the self-interest of the politicians and elected representatives of the people.

Samuel knew that if he was to have any influence at all, he needed to make the name of Samuel Colt a household word, he needed to be known and spoken of in the right circles, he needed his name in the papers.

The Boston Times had reprinted an extract from an article previously printed in the Texas Telegraph that criticised Colt's guns, not for their design but for some of the workmanship. Samuel wrote to the editor, George Roberts, demanding a full and complete retraction and threatening legal action.

Roberts protested that he had only quoted another publication, but Samuel pointed out that he had only reprinted the criticism of the gun and that the original article had actually praised the design and efficiency of the revolver. Samuel went to great lengths to explain that, although he was the inventor of the gun, he had been unable to supervise the manufacture and that unscrupulous people had produced inferior guns under his patent. He went on to say that he was, at that moment in time, making arrangements with the government for an even more remarkable invention, one that would protect America's shores from any hostile force.

Roberts was in no mood to face a suit for libel and printed the whole of the Telegraph's article. He went on to praise the distinguished character of Samuel Colt the inventor and to describe the almost miraculous properties of his submarine battery.

Other publications throughout the country added to the growing fame of Samuel Colt and the Governor of Connecticut, in an expression of pride in its talented son, made Samuel a Lieutenant Colonel in the State Militia. A proud Samuel Colt immediately had new calling cards printed that read, Colonel Samuel Colt.

Regular army officers resented Colt having the rank, but whether they liked it or not it was a valid title. The States of the Union were sovereign. Each state had its own militia and the governors had the right to commission whoever they pleased to whatever rank they liked in their militia.

Samuel used his title as often as he could in public but he never fooled himself, there is not one private letter in existence where he has signed himself Colonel Colt.

While waiting for the outcome of the election he cultivated his social standing in Washington society, getting to know as many influential people as he could and while doing so became acquainted with and befriended one Samuel F. B. Morse. Samuel had heard of Mr. Morse before, while he was seeking money from congressmen to demonstrate his revolver. Morse had been seeking funds to demonstrate his magnetic telegraph. Morse was one man who understood the principle on which Colt's submarine battery operated, although not the method of waterproofing the cable.

Samuel Finley Breese Morse, 1791 – 1872
American painter and inventor and co-developer
of Morse-code

Each man saw the potential in the other's invention but neither man regarded the other as a competitor, their end goals were quite different. Morse was hoping to make electricity a messenger of news, while Colt wanted it to become a courier of destruction. As the two men talked, they each made suggestions about the other's invention and in the search for government funds each praised the invention of the other to their mutual benefit.

Samuel, no doubt hoping that his new title of Col. Colt would carry some weight, was quick to point out that any general in the field that could communicate with his troops over a long distance, would have a considerable advantage over one who could not, and that Morse's invention, when combined with his own waterproof cable, could supply the means to do just that.

From a letter written by Samuel Morse to Joseph Henry of the college of New Jersey, it can be seen that there was a great deal of collaboration between Morse and Colt on the waterproof cable and its development. The letter reads:

"During the last few months I have availed myself of the means which Mr. Samuel Colt has had at his command in experimenting with wire circuits for testing his submarine batteries; also to test some very important matters in relation

to the Telegraph. I loaned him, in the first instance, my two reels of wire, which is reduced to eight and a quarter miles.

The experiments were highly satisfactory, the magnetism and the heating effect, which later Mr. Colt desired, being apparently stronger when the wire was stretched out than when in coil. We also found that when one wire was coated, the other might be naked, and passed to any distance.

This result induced Mr. Colt to contract for his purposes, for the purchase of forty miles of wire. Twenty miles have already been finished, and we have experimented with perfectly satisfactory results on this distance."

The occupants of the War Department, however, would just as soon believe that people could talk over a wire as send writing through it, but they were nevertheless willing to be shown that it could be done.

Congressmen were not so open to the idea, however, they needed voters to keep them in office and what Morse was proposing to do, using the power of lightning to send writing over miles of cable, sounded too much like magic. Was this man Morse in league with the devil?

Harrison was the new president and Colt's expectations rose when Daniel Webster was made Secretary of State, as he saw this as an announcement that he was going to settle the Maine boundary controversy. However, Harrison had other things on his mind, he gave the governorship of Iowa to the fiancé of his son's widow and had other friends and family lined up for other government jobs.

Realising that congress would oppose the appointments he hesitated to summon them. Without congress, Morse and Colt could get no funds and then Harrison died on April 4th after only one month in office, and Vice-President Tyler took over.

Trying to get money from government, by private individuals for undersea warfare, was never going to be easy. Government officials were sceptical of such new ideas and naval officers, who were maybe less sceptical, both recognised and feared a threat to the traditional supremacy of their wooden-hulled warships.

Samuel managed to get a meeting with Tyler and it would seem that Tyler was impressed, at least enough to have $20,000 appropriated for experiment and demonstration of Colt's submarine battery.

As soon as news reached Samuel's family of the appropriation the letters began to arrive, His father wrote asking for a few hundred dollars, brother James asked for five hundred because business was slack and he needed new clothes. Brother John had quit Cincinnati and moved to New York, bringing with him a young woman called Caroline Henshaw, who was still in her teens.

Miss Henshaw, who was originally from Germany, was known to both John and Samuel Colt and indeed, it would seem that Samuel Colt had known her first, having met in Philadelphia.

Some claim that Sam had entered into a relationship with her but had later ended it. In 1841 Caroline Henshaw left Philadelphia and moved into the house of Captain and Mrs Haff, in New York, where John Colt followed a month or so later. After John arrived, she moved into her own place at 42 Monroe Street. John Colt said that he had not lived at either house, but he does appear to have been a frequent, if somewhat secretive, visitor, as was his brother Samuel.

John Colt began referring to Caroline as his wife, presumably because her pregnancy was beginning to show, but just which of the brothers was the father of her child is difficult to know. Both men seemed to be infatuated with her and Caroline added to the mystery by at one time claiming that John could not have fathered her child and at another time saying that he was.

When John set up in New York, he had an office in the same building as Asa Wheeler, a fellow accountant who also taught students at his office. John Colt and Asa Wheeler had meet in 1838 when John had been promoting his book-keeping book in the business areas of Manhattan. John Colt had looked

Asa up when he'd been looking for office space, knowing that he was occupying two offices in the Granite Building.

This was an excellent location for John and he asked Asa to let him use one of the offices for six weeks. The arrangement was for Colt to pay ten dollars at the end of four weeks and five dollars for any additional week after that. September 4th 1841 was supposed to be the last day.

John Colt however was still occupying the office two weeks after that and showed no sign of leaving. Asa and John were frequently in and out of each other's office to chat or borrow writing supplies and after John started to outstay his welcome Asa also had to badger him for unpaid rent.

It would seem that although John had the outward appearance of being wealthy, he was unable or unwilling to pay his debts.

John wanted Samuel to finance his bookkeeping textbook. The family appear to have assumed that the government was now going to finance Samuel in all his endeavours. Samuel sent his father three hundred dollars, James a hundred and loaned John two hundred for his book venture but explained to each of them that the money he was sending was from the sale of stocks, and that he could not let them have any of the government funds.

Samuel continued to enjoy congressional favour for several years, despite the fact that former president John Quincy Adams denounced the submarine battery as an unchristian contraption.

Samuel knew that although he could successfully detonate a mine underwater, that was not the only problem that had to be solved. The mine had to be detonated when a ship was over or at least close to it. He needed an accurate system of minefield surveillance.

At first, Colt came up with the idea of operating the two observers system using visual cross-bearing coordinates. This idea had come before the observational mine system devised for the defence of Kiel harbour on the western Baltic in 1848. Colt later came up with a unique and quite remarkable single observer system, using what he referred to as a "torpedo tower."

Samuel was doing better than ever; adequate appropriations were coming his way. The government had taken a firm stance with the British over the Maine boundary dispute and had told congress that they must be prepared for conflict if diplomacy failed.

Thought of war always made elected representatives uneasy. They knew their voters and were well aware that those who shouted loudest for war, always wanted others to do the fighting and suffer the casualties. Woe to the congressman who voted for a war in which too many American sons died.

Colt's submarine battery, that could destroy the enemy without any American casualties, sounded like just what the doctor ordered.

Chapter Eight

Murder most foul

Samuel's brother John was in difficulties again, income from the sales of his bookkeeping book was meagre and he was unable to pay his printer. He was struggling even to meet living expenses and to make matters worse, Caroline was expecting and Samuel Adams, John's printer, was becoming threatening over his unpaid account.

There is a great deal of speculation that the baby Caroline was carrying, was in fact the child of Samuel Colt, but this is not proven, although the child was named Samuel after his uncle and later, Samuel took care of Caroline and her child.

Samuel would have been more than willing to help his brother with funds from his own pocket, but he was putting off some of his own creditors and was determined not to dip into government funds to pay Adams. He urged John to come to some amicable arrangement with Adams. A decision that Samuel was later to deeply regret.

Samuel Adams disappeared on September 17th 1841.

Asa Wheeler, John's landlord, said that on that day he was giving a lesson to one Arzac Seignette, a student of his, when they heard noises like the clashing of sabres followed by a loud boom coming from down the hallway towards Colt's room. Asa didn't think Colt was in that day, being under the impression that he had gone to Philadelphia on business. Arzac said later, that the noise sounded like a man being thrown to the floor.

Asa Wheeler and his student went down the hall to Colt's office, which was locked and Wheeler got down on his knee and looked through the keyhole. At first, he could see nothing because the drop was down, covering the keyhole and blocking his view.

Taking his pen from his pocket he inserted the pointed end through the keyhole and was able to push the drop to one side.

Escutcheon with dust cover

Keyholes in those days often had drop dust covers over them to prevent dirt and grime getting into the lock mechanism as shown here.

This time when he looked in, with the cover pushed aside, he saw a shadowy figure in shirt sleeves bending down over something on the floor by the west wall. On the table were two black hats. As Asa was watching the figure inside, whom he was unable to identify because he couldn't see his face, stood up and placed something on the table, before returning to the same spot as before.

The man's behaviour inside the room, together with the noises they had heard, made Asa think that something very strange had taken place inside Colt's office.

Asa instructed his student to stay and watch Colt's door while he went to find the building's owner. When he returned, he had a man with him who Arzac referred to as Mr Oakland. Arzac reported to them that no one had entered or exited Colt's office and they were then joined by another couple of students and one John Delnous, a man who had been hoping to rent John Colt's office when he vacated.

They decided to send for the police.

At that time the New York police consisted of an assorted group of citizens protecting their own property, some angry vigilantes and a small, largely untrained group of marshals, constables and watchmen. It was not an organised force as we think of it today and nobody came, so eventually they all left.

The last to leave were John Delnous and Asa Wheeler who sat and listened from Asa's office for a while, but deciding that there was probably no longer anybody in Colt's office and that there was nothing they could do, they left.

According to John Delnous, he returned later and listened for another half an hour, but it is unclear if he told Asa at the time of his return to his office. He states that as he sat in the office with the door ajar, he heard someone unlock Colt's office door, exit, lock it again and leave. He waited a while and then heard footsteps returning and someone entering the office again. Delnous then claims that he went down and listened at the door and that he could hear the sounds of someone cleaning with a pail of water and the sounds of scrubbing.

Delnous slept in Asa's office that night and was awakened in the morning, he says, by the sounds of sawing and nailing. When he listened at Colt's door the sounds stopped so he grabbed his hat and coat and went out for breakfast.

When Delnous returned to the Granite Building an hour later, Law Octon, the keeper of the building was there and they both saw John Colt emerge from his office.

There was a crate on the landing, and Colt dragged it to the top of the stairs where he proceeded to let it slide down, going first and using his shoulders to prevent it descending too fast.

John Delnous asked Colt what had been going on in his office the previous night and Colt answered by saying that the key was in the lock, and that he should, *"Go and look."*

Outside in Chambers street, Colt left the crate on a cart near the entrance to the Granite Building and enlisted the help of Richard Barstow a haulier, who was waiting in his carriage at the corner of Church and Chambers.

Colt and Barstow took the crate to the docks and loaded it onto a ship bound for New Orleans.

Docked in New York harbour that day was the cargo ship Kalamazoo. It had been scheduled to sail some days earlier but a heatwave had closed a lot of businesses in the city and she was waiting in port until business and weather returned to normal.

On Sunday morning September 26th 1841, nine days after Adams disappearance and the odd goings on at Colt's office, one of the crew ran to fetch the captain, a man called Hawke, who was drinking at Lovejoy's Hotel.

Some crew had located the source of a foul stench coming from the hold of the ship. The crate from which the terrible smell was coming was addressed to R. P. Gross, in care of Mr. Gray, in St. Louis, Missouri.

Captain Hawke gave the order for the crate to be opened. The stench was so overwhelming that several of the men walked off the ship. Inside was the body of a man, later identified as that of Samuel Adams.

The story was of course sensationalised in the newspapers, rumours abounded, and the details of the strange goings on at Colt's office became common knowledge. John Colt was then arrested for the murder of Samuel Adams.

The crew of the Kalamazoo were quite naturally reluctant to remove the body from the crate so it was decided to spread some "chloride of lime" over the corpse, nail it shut again and transport it to the city's dead house (Morgue).

Abner Milligan was the deputy coroner and as soon as he viewed the partly decomposed and badly beaten body, he called in the help of two local Doctors, Dr. Gilman and Dr. Kissam.

When the body was lifted from the crate it was seen to have been hogtied and the skull was fractured in several places. Gillman described the head injuries as having been caused by an object that was round in shape but also sharp.

A search of John Colt's office turned up a hatchet that had an axe head on one side and a ball peen hammer shape on the other, which all agreed was most probably the murder weapon.

Thomas Taylor, one of the magistrate's chief investigators, went to John Colt's address and the door was opened he said, by a beautiful, young and obviously pregnant woman who called herself Mrs. Colt. This was of course Caroline Henshaw who had come to New York with John.

Taylor asked to see John's trunk. In those days a man who travelled as John did, would have kept all his documents and valuable possessions in his trunk. Taylor asked Caroline for the key but she said she would not open it without John being there. Taylor had the trunk taken, with Caroline, to the police office where he had John brought from his cell to witness the opening.

Caroline opened the trunk in the presence of the Mayor, Taylor and John Colt. Inside the trunk the men found an expensive gold watch. Taylor asked John who the watch belonged to, thinking it was an expensive item for John to own, seeing as how he was so low on funds.

John claimed that the watch was his but Taylor didn't believe him. He asked John who had made the watch and where had he bought it and when. A watch was an important purchase for a man back then, and Taylor was sure that if the watch really did belong to John Colt, he would know these things, but John could not recall where he had bought it.

Taylor enquired of local watchmakers to see if he could trace the seller but having no luck there, he showed the watch to Mrs Emmeline Adams, the widow of the dead man.

Emmeline identified the watch as one belonging to her murdered husband and stated, *"I was in the country when he got it, and had been gone four to five weeks. The watch had been the subject of conversation. He sat on the foot of the bed on Wednesday, took the key off my chain and endeavoured with the pinchers to get the dents out. He was at 90 Chatham Street Wednesday night with me and had it."*

John Colt was arraigned by a grand jury on Tuesday September 28th 1841. John pleaded not guilty and pledged to fight the charges with everything he had. The trial was set for early the following year. After contemplating his position and talking to his lawyers John announced that he was willing to give a full and detailed account of what had transpired between himself and Samuel Adams on that fateful night.

According to John Colt, it had been between three and four o'clock in the afternoon on Friday September 17th when Samuel Adams had arrived at the office John rented from Asa Wheeler at The Granite Building. John had been working on some accounts and something in the calculations had stumped him. Adams, he said, just strode into the room and sat in the chair facing John without speaking a word.

There had been a difference of opinion between the two men regarding what Adams regarded as an unpaid bill. John pointed out to Adams that the bill he had given John had been wrong. John had received the bill some ten or twelve days earlier and that had given him plenty of time to go over it to see where Adams had made a mistake. John then gave Adams a copy of how the bill should have looked. Adams took the paper and studied it.

John said that he had hoped that was the end of the matter, but instead Samuel screamed, *"you lied, I was right the first time, you are trying to cheat me!"*

According to John, both men then stood and Samuel Adams was in a rage and struck John across his mouth and nose, causing his nose to bleed. John struck his assailant back inciting even more anger in Adams.

John stated that at the time, he was wearing a businessman's suit with a cravat that was tied in a necktie knot. Adams then grabbed John by his cravat and pushing him up against the wall behind his desk he twisted it tight, so that John was scarce able to breath.

Laying on the table beside John was a hammer with an axe on one side and a ball-peen hammer on the other. In desperation, John claimed that he grabbed hold of the hammer and struck Adams over the head. *"Then a strange feeling of disconnect came upon me and I lost all power of reason."* He later told his lawyers.

John Colt was portraying the fateful events of that day as ones of spontaneous self-defence, he claimed he had little memory of what occurred after he first struck Adams, suggesting that his mind had been affected by lack of oxygen due to being strangled with his cravat.

After the deed was done John was at a loss as to what to do next. Blood was streaming from Adams's head and pooling on the floor. John took some string that had been around some boxes and tied this tightly around Adams's neck in an attempt t stop the bleeding. He had by this time decided to dispose of the body and it was at this time that he decided to strip Adams of his clothing, in case he could be identified by it, and rolled his body in an awning.

John needed to think, so he went to the park to clear his head. He said that at one time he considered burning down the building where his office was, it would be a solution to his immediate problem but on reflection he realised that there was too much risk of others being killed in the fire, so he returned to his office. When he got back to his office, a safer and much more practical solution occurred to him.

John obtained a crate and realising that Adams would not fit inside the crate in the posture in which he had died John used some of the awning cord and hog-tied the body so that it would fit.

After stuffing Adams's body into the crate, he also put in his clothes and the towels that he had used to mop up the blood, and nailed it shut. The Washington Bath House was just around the corner on Pearl Street and John went there to clean up before going home to Caroline at 42 Monroe Street.

The following morning he was up early and when he arrived at his office he was relieved to find everything just as he had left it. He was unaware at that time that Asa Wheeler was convinced something sinister had occurred the previous evening and had already been to the police.

Having satisfied himself that all was well, he went to Wood's General store to buy nails to finish sealing the crate and then walked down to the East River to ascertain which ships were leaving. Finding that the Kalamazoo was about ready to sail he quickly returned to his office, finished nailing up the crate and addressed it to a fictitious address. He managed to get the crate to the top of the stairs by himself but needed help to get down the stairs to the road and from there to the docks. He went outside and enlisted the help of a haulier. With the help of the haulier he loaded the crate onto the Kalamazoo.

After his exertions he called into Lovejoy's hotel for coffee and a roll before returning once again to his office, where he spent a large part of the morning cleaning blood from the floor. He was physically and mentally exhausted by the time he returned home.

When he got to the apartment, that he shared with Caroline, he said he was weary and was going back to bed. Caroline noticed scratches and bruising on John's neck and asked him what had happened but he said he was in no mood to talk.

All the time after his arrest John continued saying that he had acted in self-defence, but many asked why, if that was the case, that he only made his confession after his arrest.

In one of the interviews he gave after his arrest he said, *"This man. who came here a few minutes since and insulted me is dead, dead by my hand. I did not mean to kill him, but he is dead. He would have slain me, or he would have proclaimed a triumph over me, and he perished in the attempt at one or the other, neither of which could I have brooked. Shall I rush forth and proclaim the truth? But suppose I do, will it be believed? Throughout my entire life I have been doomed to one series of misconstructions."*

Samuel Colt was horrified by what he described in his letters to James as *"John's misfortunes."* The publicity the case was receiving in the papers was damaging to Samuel's business but there is no sign that he ever contemplated abandoning his brother, indeed, Samuel bore the brunt of the cost of John's defence.

The papers were against John Colt and portrayed him as a womaniser and a gambler, and of course there is some truth in that, but they really went to town on him, digging into every aspect of his past life. They said he lied to get into the Marines and falsified documents to get out and they published lurid stories about his affair with a slave. The possibility that he was innocent or had acted in self-defence was never discussed.

Samuel hired Robert Emmet, the son of Thomas Addis Emmet and John Morrill, two of the most respected members of the New York bar, to head his brother's defence. He gave them each one thousand dollars as a retainer and ten shares in the Submarine Battery Company. Later each was to receive some extra shares, both in the Submarine Battery Company and Samuel's Waterproof Cable Company.

Because of the newspaper's portrayal of John Colt as a womaniser and gambler, public opinion was generally against him, maybe not so much for the killing itself, which if done in self-defence they could maybe understand, but for the way he acted after in cleaning up the evidence and going to the bathhouse to wash, then going back the next day and disposing of the body.

John was not without visitors in prison however, Caroline Henshaw visited every day and Howard Payne the famous playwright and producer was seen to visit on occasion. Howard Payne is probably best remembered for writing "Home Sweet Home." Also seen visiting John's cell in the Tombs were Lewis Gaylord Clark, the editor of the Knickerbocker magazine as well as the celebrated author Edgar Allen Poe. Poe's story "The Oblong Box," is partially based on the murder of Samuel Adams.

At the trial, Morrill, acting for the defence, spoke to the jury and the court, *"A man will fight for his life, and the counsel will contend not only for that life but for justice to the prisoner. It is with this feeling, and not with the vie to detain the jury, that we have been thus minute.*

"Gentlemen, John C. Colt, poor and friendless, a fellow citizen, comes before charged with crime. He comes before you in defence of that life which is dear to all. He askes you to mete him out justice...it is all he asks; it is all we ask. We seek but one thing: It is that we may have mercy according to law, and if he has such, we have no doubt that he will find a safe deliverance at your hands."

At one time the prosecution, for reasons that are unclear, tried to say that one of Samuel Colt's revolvers had also been used to kill Adams. Now Wheeler had described the noise he heard as being like the clash of sabres, so the prosecution put forward that the bullet or ball had been fired from the gun under force of the percussion cap charge only.

Selden and Morrill called Samuel Colt to give evidence and he was asked to demonstrate the firing of a ball from his gun using only a percussion cap. There was a load boom, but Samuel was able to catch the ball in his hand. He then fired the gun in the same manner at an open book held a few paces away. The ball penetrated nine pages, exactly the same number as were penetrated when he threw the ball at the book by hand, thus disproving the prosecutions assertions, there was no way a ball would have penetrated the deceased head if fired in that manner.

The trial then took a rather gruesome turn as the prosecution asked for the head of the murdered Mr. Adams to be brought into court and shown to the jury, along with the axe, and despite Selden's objections this was done and the jury was shown how the axe exactly fitted the wound in the skull.

The defence had never denied that the hammer come axe had been the weapon used, so the only reason the prosecution could possibly have had for such a bizarre request was for sensationalism and to horrify the jury and turn them against John Colt.

Caroline Henshaw, who had recently given birth to her baby, a boy named Samuel, after his supposed uncle, was called to give evidence. She was regarded by the audience and the jury alike as little more than a prostitute, living in sin with a man of low morals and now accused of a gruesome murder.

If the jury had been aware of the possibility that Samuel Colt had fathered her child, rather than the man she was living with, they would no doubt have convicted John Colt on the spot and hung him there and then.

Caroline was asked about her relationship with the prisoner and she replied sharply that she was *"made mother by Mr. Colt."* She did not identify which Mr. Colt and there was no reason at this time to question which she meant.

She stated that she and John Colt had a regular routine, that when he arrived home from work, generally a little after nine-thirty, they would go for a walk before retiring for the night. She said, however, that on the night in question he had arrived home late, and appeared to be in a mild state of mania. She said that later that night she had seen black bruises and scratches around his neck and it looked to her as if he had been in some kind of skirmish. She also said that he slept with his nightshirt buttoned up to the neck that night and for two nights following, which was not his normal practise.

This evidence was good support for John's assertion of self-defence, but it is doubtful that the jury gave it much credence because of their low opinion of Caroline herself.

Selden had planned to call several character witnesses to vouch for Caroline's credibility and good standing, saying, *"My client's relation with her was one of the acts for which he has been called by public sentiment to answer, but she was no prostitute except as regard to him. He did wrong and she did. But adverse circumstances alone caused them to live together in the illegitimate manner they did."*

Judge Kent refused to allow any of Selden's character witnesses to testify on Caroline's behalf, stating, *"Unless the character of a witness is impeached, the testimony should be disallowed. It is unnecessary to produce evidence as to the character of the last witness."*

After the prosecution and the defence had made their summations to the jury, Judge Kent addressed them. He asked them to, *"Do away with the excitement thrown around the case by the speeches of council. Some allusion has been made to the excitement out of doors,"* he said, pointing in the direction of the gallery and those who clambered to see John Colt die at the end of a noose. *"I am inclined to believe it is overrated. Had I not thought so, I would have postponed the trial. It would have been strange if, in the city of New York, the public mind would not have been shocked by the murder, but I have no doubt that every justice has been done to the prisoner. The Court has kept everything uninfluenced by contamination from without, and I have no doubt but reliance can be had upon the sound heads before us. I was sorry to find some acerbity of feeling shown among the council, but I see no occasion for it. Never have I known more talent or industry displayed than in this cause. No blame is deserved on either side, and as to the District Attorney he has discharged his duty ably and eloquently, and without any feeling but that of duty."*

He then gave a long talk to the jury about the law, explaining that there were four grades of homicide, justifiable homicide, excusable homicide, manslaughter and murder.

He explained that there is little difference between the grades of the first two, one being where an officer kills in the performance of their duty and the other is where a man kills in defence of his life.

He instructed the jury, *"If you think Colt killed Adams to protect himself from an attempt at murder or felony he is justified and no blame is attached to the prisoner."*

He went on, *"You may say that Colt designed to take Adam's life, if so, it was murder. But you must show premeditation. This is not necessary to have been previous to Adams going into his room. If you think he did it, not in hot blood, or in a fracas, it is murder. But if you do not think such, it is manslaughter, and you must bring it within one of the grades."*

Despite a brilliant defence and the appearance of Howard Payne and Gaylord Clark as character witnesses, John Caldwell Colt was found guilty of murder in the first degree and was sentenced to be hanged in the Tombs prison yard on 18th November 1842.

The verdict was perhaps inevitable, John Colt had been tried and found guilty in the newspapers long before the trial proper. It seems obvious that when he killed Samuel Adams he acted in self-defence and the actions he took afterwards were because he panicked, afraid that he would not be believed because of his lifestyle. It is also clear that he was found guilty of murder, largely because of the lengths he went to in hiding the body and covering up the evidence, after the event.

The execution was scheduled for four o' clock in the afternoon. A little before noon on that day, Caroline Henshaw was brought to John's cell and with Samuel Colt and some friends as witnesses, she was married to John Caldwell Colt.

After the wedding a few friends and family, such as Payne, Emmet and cousin Dudley Seldon, came to say their goodbyes to John and departed a little before three o' clock.

Soon after, those who had been invited to watch the hanging began to gather in the prison yard, and a crowd of several thousand surrounded the outside of the Tombs.

Artists depiction of the wedding of John Colt and
Caroline in the Tombs prison New York 1842.
© Charles Sutton 1874

Half an hour before the execution was due to take place, a fire broke out in the cupola of the prison. A cupola is tall dome-like structure on the top of a building, used either as a lookout post or to admit light and air. The fire caused pandemonium, some visitors to the prison ran out in panic and when the fire-engines arrived, the crowd outside were shrieking and jeering and some even tried to burst into the prison in the wake of the fire-engines. All thought of the grim business at hand was forgotten until the fire was put out.

The original Egyptian-Revival-style Tombs building in an etching from 1870. Notice the cupola is missing, having been destroyed in the fire of 1842.

After the flames were extinguished but with smoke still hanging in the air, the prison guards went to fetch John Colt from his cell, only to find him dead in his cot, apparently stabbed through the heart.

The newspapers had a field day. Even after the trial was over and the sentence pronounced the newspapers had continued to print unsubstantiated stories about escape attempts and bribes being paid to officials. The news of his death brought a whole new round of theories and conjecture. Did John Colt commit suicide by stabbing himself in the heart or had he in fact escaped from prison during the confusion caused by the fire?

The sheriff in charge of the Tombs at the time turned over to the city a bribe of $1,000 that he claimed he had received from an anonymous person, along with a promise of another $1,000 if Colt escaped.

Some have put forward the theory that the bribe was from Samuel Colt, but it is clear from Samuel's letters that he was in no position to hand out thousand dollar bribes.

Others suspect that the editor of the Herald newspaper, Mr. James Gordon Bennett, would have reaped huge circulation benefits if Colt had escaped only to be apprehended again by agents of the newspaper. Did John Colt suspect betrayal at the last minute and kill himself? It is clear however, from Samuel's writings that the speculations about a last-minute escape are entirely baseless.

James Gordon Bennett
1795 – 1872
Born in Newmill, Scotland he sailed to America in 1819.

Samuel's first concern after his brother's death was to get Caroline and her new-born son, named Samuel after his uncle, out of New York.

He corresponded several times with his brother James on the subject of what should become of her. In the end Samuel wrote saying that he had found a solution and that the solution would relieve the family from constantly being reminded of, "*John's misfortune.*" None of the letters, however, actually say what the solution was. The only clue comes from a statement that, "*She speaks and understands German and can best be cared for in the German countries.*" He later tells James that he has made all the necessary arrangements.

What actually happened to Caroline and the young Samuel Colt is something of a mystery after that, certainly

Caroline Colt is never heard from again in America, although there are reports of a Miss Julia Leicester turning up in various German cities with a young child called Samuel Colt. They are described as nephew and niece and wards of Colonel Samuel Colt.

Chapter Nine

Harbour Defence

While Samuel was working hard supporting his brother's defence, he was also beavering away promoting his submarine battery.

By now Samuel had abandoned his two-observer system in favour of a single observer one. This consisted of a tall, "torpedo tower" in which an observer would be located. Within this observation post would be a ten-foot convex mirror, positioned above and behind the observer in order to reflect an image of the minefield onto a mirrored grid before him.

Embedded in this grid would be numerous metallic terminals, each one positioned on the grid's equivalent of the position of one of Colt's mines and each terminal would have a cable connection to its corresponding mine. Colt envisaged his operator being able to trigger the detonation of selected clusters of mines as the reflected image of an enemy warship moved across the grid.

This revolutionary concept had, however, two weaknesses, fog and darkness. These weaknesses would eventually necessitate the incorporation of contact detonators in any effective observation mine system.

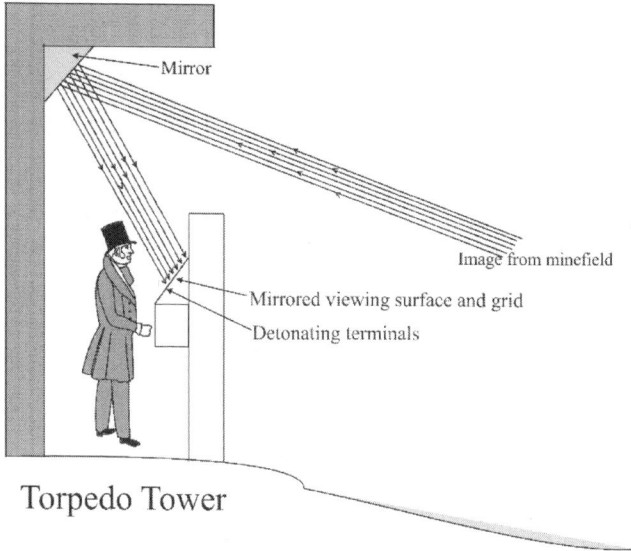

Torpedo Tower

Colt was not the only one working on new ways of harbour defence at that time. Robert L. Stevens was working on his "harbour defence battery," and had received $250,000 for what was referred to as a "revolutionary iron-hulled Stevens Battery." The machine resembled a metal submersible canoe and was able to submerge herself to her gunwales to make her a smaller target and speed towards an enemy ship.

After the collapse of the Paterson Arms Company, Samuel himself was in dire need of funds, so he wrote to President Tylor.

"Sir

It is with no little diffidence that I venture to submit the following for your consideration, feeling as I do that its apparent extravagance may prevent you from paying t that attention which it merits; and but for the duty I owe my country in these threatening times, I should still longer delay making this communication.

For more than ten years past I have employed my leisure in study and experiment to perfect the invention of which I now consider myself master; and which, if adopted for the service of our Government, will not only save them millions of outlay for the construction of means of defence, but in the event of foreign war, it will prove a perfect safeguard against all the combined fleets of Europe, with out exposing the lives of our citizens.

There seems to prevail at this time with all parties a sense of the importance of effectually protecting our sea-coast; and as economy is a primary consideration in the present exhausted state of our treasury, I think I have a right to expect a favourable consideration of the propositions which I have determined to make.

By referring to the Navy State Papers, page 211, you will discover that Robert Fulton made experiments proving that a certain quantity of gunpowder discharged under the bottom of a ship would produce her instant destruction. That discovery laid the foundation for my present plan of harbour defence; and notwithstanding the failure of Fulton to use his invention to much advantage in its imperfect condition, during the last war, one glance at what he did perform is sufficient to convince the most incredulous, that if his engine could be brought under easy and safe control, it must prove an irresistible barrier against foreign invasion.

Discoveries since Fulton's time combined with an invention original with myself, enable me to effect the instant destruction of either ships or steamers at my pleasure, on their entering a harbour, whether singly or in whole fleets; while those vessels to which I am disposed to allow a passage are secure from a possibility of being injured. All this I can do while myself in perfect security, and without giving an invading enemy the slightest sign of his danger.

The whole expense of protecting a harbour like that of New York would be less than the cost of a single steamship; and when the apparatus is once prepared, one single man is sufficient to manage the destroying agent against any fleet that Europe can send.

With the above statements as an intimation of what can be done, I will mention in as brief a manner as possible the terms on which I will make an exhibition, to prove to yourself and your Cabinet that a sailing vessel or steamboat cannot pass (without permission) either in or out of a harbour where my engines of destruction are employed.

To make the exhibition (which I contemplate, should I meet with sufficient encouragement) will require an expenditure of $20,000, which sum I will employ for that purpose from my own means, on condition that the Government will lend me such aid as I shall require (which can be supplied without incurring new expenses), and that when I get through my exhibition the Government shall refund to me all my money which I shall have expended, and pay me an annual sum as a premium for my secret.

I hope I may be excused from mentioning that, as any hint of my plans at this time must prove prejudicial, it is my wish that the present communication may be kept from the view of all persons excepting the members of your Cabinet. I have the honour to be, Sir, most respectfully,

Your Excellency's devoted
And obedient servant
Samuel Colt

Although some people such as Senator Samuel L. Southard of New Jersey, were supporting bills for the appropriation of money for the development of Colt's invention, one assumes because he had faith in it and was acting patriotically rather than because Samuel had given him some shares in the company, Colt still felt that it would be better if the invention caught the public's imagination.

To this end, and now with government approval, he organised a number of demonstrations off Coney Island and in Upper New York Bay. Newspaper reports of the demonstrations of a device that could protect the country without endangering American lives met with great public approval, assuring Colt of large crowds for his demonstrations.

After a number of small-scale demonstrations, the government agreed to let Samuel have an obsolete gunboat, the "Boxer." The idea was to put an end to the idea held by many senior officers, that it was one thing to cause an underwater explosion that sent a jet of water into the air, it was quite another to blow up a warship. These same officers made no secret of the fact that they mistrusted Samuel, and they wondered if the showman might be sneaky enough to plant time-bombs aboard the Boxer.

The demonstration was carried out under the close supervision of the navy on 4th July 1842, thirteen years after Samuel had caused his first explosion on Ware Pond.

The Boxer was anchored well out in the harbour off Castle Garden and long before the time set for the explosion large crowds had gathered to watch.

Still suspecting some kind of underhand shenanigans, the navy thoroughly inspected the vessel for time-bombs and insisted that they would decide the exact time the mine would be detonated. The navy left men on board the Boxer for over an hour after Samuel had signalled that all was ready. Had Samuel indeed set time-bombs under the ship, there would most certainly have been a terrible tragedy that day.

The crowd was now becoming impatient, so the men aboard the Boxer took to their boats and came ashore. When they were at a safe distance the navy gave the order for Samuel, who was aboard another ship some two miles away, to fire his mine.

After the smoke had cleared, what was left of the Boxer was floating with the tide, and any resemblance she once had to something to be feared was gone forever. Soon after the demonstration Samul received a letter from John Mount of Jersey City dated 6th July 1842.

"I cannot refrain from writing you my congratulations on the entire success of your recent submarine explosion. I witnessed it, among hundreds, from the lower wharf of Jersey City. As the dense volume of smoke rose heavenward, its

terrific grandeur could only be exceeded by the amazement and wonder of all the multitude around me at the means by which it was accomplished. Its altitude in a line of vision from where I stood, was far above the royal truck of the British Frigate, Warspite, consequently must have been very high. I trust, my dear sir, that the government will properly appreciate the vast importance of this mode of defence and that you may reap the honours and emoluments to which you are justly entitled."

Thine in sincerity,

John Mount

In usual Colt style, Samuel had sent invitations to several people from the New York media, some of whom he had met during his brother's trial. Several papers gave a good account of the demonstration with possibly the best being given by the Evening Post.

"Colt's sub-marine battery created attention, and was witnessed by many thousands with great satisfaction. An old hulk was moored off Castle Garden fitted with temporary masts, from which were displayed various flags, with piratical devices, immediately under which the battery was placed, and the effect of the explosion was tremendous. The vessel was shattered into fragments, some of which were thrown two or

three hundred feet in the air, and there was not a single piece left longer than a man could have carried in one hand."

Navy officers however, continued to be sceptical, and another trial was carried out on the eighteenth of October 1842, when the three-hundred-ton brig "Volta" was blown out of the water by one of Samuel's mines. This experiment was conducted under the patronage of the American Institute in connection with their annual exhibition.

Still, Commodore Perry voiced the view that, *"Blowing up a vessel at anchor is no proof that one can wreck a craft under full sail and competently handled."*

In reply Colt declared, *"I will guarantee to fortify every port upon the Seaboard against the combined Fleets of Europe, at a cost for each, less than that required to build a single steam ship of war, and when once fixed, my engine of destruction may be used without the expense of fuel or soldiers, the cost of which, every year, exceeds the expense of making permanent Fortifications of my construction."*

With many differing view and arguments being passed backwards and forwards, it was proposed that Samuel should destroy a vessel as it sailed down the Potomac, and after some searching, a schooner was provided.

Commodore Perry wanted the ship to be fully crewed so that they could undertake to navigate the ship through Colt's minefield. He suggested that Congress appropriate fifty thousand dollars and that the money should go to Samuel if he blew the vessel up and the sailors if he failed. He said that if Samuel succeeded, he would deserve the money and the sailors would not need it.

Samuel was horrified by the suggestion and sought help from his friend Samuel Morse, who understood the principle of the mine. Morse managed to make it plain to Washington that any attempt to send a fully-manned ship through Colt's minefield would leave Colt in the unenviable position of having to either admit to an inefficiency that did not exist, or of committing wholesale murder. After some further discussion it was decided that the crew should abandon the ship shortly before it entered the minefield, and the trial was set for 13th April 1844.

On hand to view the demonstration this time was none other than President John Tyler, the first vice-president to take office after the death of a serving president.

After all the sailors had abandoned the schooner it drifted unimpeded for a while and the sceptical among the officers must have been feeling justified in their beliefs, however, there was then a burst of flame and spray and for a while the schooner was hidden in smoke. When the smoke cleared a large patch of flotsam occupied the area of water where the schooner had been. The demonstration had been an enormous success.

Samuel Colt was invited aboard the presidential yacht by President Tylor, where he was presented with a bouquet of flowers. The bouquet contained roses, pansies and cedar and they were found, carefully pressed and labelled in one of Colt's scrapbooks after his death.

The Niles National Register described the incident, *"A steamer containing the President and members of the cabinet, with their suits, was opposite the spectators, and its illustrious and precious freight received a very hearty greeting from the mouths of twenty-four guns. A few minutes afterwards the signal for the explosion was given by the discharge of a twenty-four pounder, and instantaneously as though a missile from the gun itself had born the torch to a magazine in her, the old craft was sent in ten million of fragments five hundred feet into the air, and then fell into the water with a roar like that of Niagara."*

Only two people still opposed the submarine battery, John Quincy Adams in Congress and Lieutenant Colonel Joseph J. Totten. There is no mystery as to why Adams was against the invention, he disliked Colt intensely and was totally opposed to, *"killing men by infernal contraptions on the bottom of the sea."* He believed that the mass murder of war should be accomplished by methods which are sanctified by precedent as properly orthodox.

His views were not shared by others studying Samuel's invention however, who failed to see why sending men to their deaths with a single blast from the sea, was more cruel and inhumane than piecing them with wooden splinters, scalding them to death with boiling pitch, searing them with red hot shot, hacking them to death with a cutlass or trapping them in a burning hulk, which were the more conventional practices of the day. They had high regard for Mr. Adams but disagreed with him completely on this issue.

Colonel Totten's opposition however, is more difficult to understand. He had served with Simon Bernard, who had been Lieutenant General of engineers under Napoleon and was generally regarded as a progressive officer. He had constructed works at Newport and elsewhere that marked a new era in coastal defence planning. Colt's mine should have fitted in well with Totten's system but he was vehemently opposed to it.

John Quincy Adams
1767-1848
American president 1825-1829

Joseph J. Totten
1788-1864
Chief of Engineers

Unfortunately for Samuel, Totten's opinions carried a lot of weight in both the army and the navy, even to the extent that those who were enthusiastic about Colt's mines, began to doubt their own judgement.

Samuel continued to demonstrate his mine, but when the Ashburton Treaty was signed settling the boundary dispute, he realised that the chance of a government contract was slipping from his grasp.

Colt made arrangements for one final demonstration of his submarine battery at Washington. Shortly before Colt's demonstration on the 28th February 1844 the capital had been shocked by the Princeton disaster.

An accident had occurred during an ordnance demonstration aboard the new steam-frigate "Princeton," while cruising on the Potomac near Mount Vernon. On board at the time was President Tyler and his entourage to witness a test firing of Captain Robert F. Stockton's 12-inch Peacemaker cannon. The gun exploded, almost killing the president and claiming the lives of five members of the presidential party, including the newly appointed Secretary of State Abel P. Upshur, who was the only member of the government familiar with the secret of Colt's Battery.

The Princeton Disaster 1844

Samuel was supplied with anchors, boats, timber and mooring lines from the Washington Navy Yard as well as charts of the Potomac and Eastern Branch rivers above Alexandria. On 1st April Samuel reported to, Representative

Henry A. Wise, that he had fortified the river leading to the Navy Yard and that the ship is to be got under way with full sail. The ship in question, the Brunette, had been renamed the Styx, for her final cruise

The demonstration was announced in the press for thirteenth April 1844 with strict warnings about the danger to the curious and small boats in the vicinity.

The timing of the demonstration was perfect for Colt. The National Institute for the Promotion of science had convened the first major literary and scientific convention held in the United States. A week long meeting of leading scientists, it was an opportunity for inventors such as Colt and Morse to show off their inventions.

Lieutenant Junius Boyle of the Navy Yard had, on this occasion, volunteered to command the target vessel to the minefield's vicinity. It was arranged that Colt would signal his readiness with a gunshot and Boyle would respond by lowering the topsail three times. After removing the national ensign Boyle and his small crew would abandon the target vessel and leave in a small boat. When clear of the vessel they would fire a signal rocket.

Samuels first explosion was a little too early and failed to destroy the Styx, as it surly would have done if fired a minute later.

"He has missed," the crowd shouted.

His second explosion also missed but was closer than the first.

This time some boos could be heard among the shouts from the watching crowd, but then a third explosion threw wooden splinters high into the air and the Styx was split in two.

One report in the papers read, *"The shores resounded with heartfelt plaudits, subsiding into long continuing murmurs of admiration. The gratification was unbounded. Nothing could have been more completely successful. There was no accident, no injury, no disappointment in any respect; the public expectation was not met but surpassed; and when the boat containing the crew darted swiftly to the wreak, and with some difficulty restored the stripes and stars to their former station, it required no stretch of the imagination to fancy that we beheld a captive invader, which had been compelled to strike, and was now taken possession of as lawful prize."*

Colt's last demonstration. The Styx.

painting by Antoine Placide Gilbert 1844

Colt explained that he had been hampered in his efforts and was unable to proceed further because a number of small boats had come close and from his position could not be distinguished from pieces of the wreck. Colt was thus reluctant to proceed further for fear of a fatal accident.

It would seem from these comments that Colt himself was not completely happy with the outcome, but he was the only one.

The location from which Colt observed his minefield and detonated his mines is unknown, he was very secretive about his observation post locations in all his demonstrations.

His papers shed no light on the enigma either, for they contain no evidence that he purchased or used either a reflecting mirror or control grid in his destruction of the Styx.

Days after the sinking of the Styx he told the secretary of the navy, John Mason, that he had been positioned on the opposite bank of the river more than two miles distant.

If this was indeed the case, then it was remarkable. But where was the proof? If true, then Samuel would surely be successful in selling his submarine battery to the government, but there were no witnesses to prove Samuel's location at the time of the explosions.

The fact that nobody could bear witness to where Colt was at the time of any of his demonstrations and the fact that there is no evidence he purchased any of the components needed for his torpedo tower, means that even today, there is speculation about just how he achieved what he did.

Still military professionals, denied the opportunity to monitor Colt's arrangements closely were sceptical. The Army and Navy Chronicle and scientific Repository concluded in its brief notice; *"as experiments, these, as many others have been, were very beautiful and striking, but in the practical application of this apparatus to purposes of war, we have no confidence."*

As a footnote, the wreck of the Styx, despite repeated demolition efforts, continued to obstruct the narrow approach channel and gradually built up a sandbar that interfered with ship movements in and out of the yard right up until the start of the civil war.

Samuel now realised that he was never going to win, so he made an attempt to be paid for the demonstrations he had put on, he argued that officials had given him the go-ahead to conduct the demonstrations in the first place.

Samuel's arguments with government continued with Washington arguing that if Samuel's claims were genuine, then where was his patent?

Then, to everyone's surprise on 8th June 1844 Samuel submitted a formal patent application. He may have used other people's ideas to construct his mines and the way they were suspended under the water, but the torpedo tower was his and his alone.

The conclusion of the committee deciding whether to allow Colt's patent to be funded and fully backed by the United States government was that Samuel Colt had never proven that he had ever used a tower in any of his demonstrations, and that, although the invention was entitled to the favourable consideration of the government, there was not sufficient evidence before the committee to enable them to judge of the propriety of adopting it as a means of fortification; and they are therefore not prepared to recommend it for that purpose.

Seeing how the future was looking, Samuel decided to point out to the world that the secret of his success lay not so much in the mine itself but in the waterproof cable that delivered the charge. He looked for other ways in which his cable could be employed. He contacted Morse, suggesting that it would be beneficial to have his telegraph wires protected underground rather than stuck up in the air on poles and even suggested that waterways such as the Erie Canal could carry the trunk lines of his telegraph. Morse however was intent on having his wires on poles.

Chapter Ten

The Telegraph and Trouble
In Texas

By 1843 Colt was manufacturing his waterproof cable in considerable quantity and was carrying out experiments with conductors at New York University. It's clear that Colt thought that Morse's invention was destined to become a huge industry and he wanted to be in a position to become its main supplier of materials.

By the middle of 1844 Colt had obtained rights from Morse to construct a telegraph line linking Coney Island, New York, Brooklyn and Jersey. For this he was to pay $800, half when the line was built and the rest in instalments after it was put into operation.

In 1845 Samuel, together with a book dealer called William Robinson and several others, organised and incorporated the New York and Offing Magnetic Telegraph Association.

Samuel's associates were to supply the cash. Samuel was to be paid fifty dollars a mile for the use of his wire, the payment to be made in stock of the corporation.

As well as paying the fifty dollars a mile for the use of the wire the company agreed to pay for it and to finance all the construction work. Samuel also received a commission on any stock he sold and an additional commission for all customers he brought to the company.

An observation tower was built on Coney Island and a telegraph wire run to Dorr's Granite Building in the rear of Merchants' Exchange. For a fee of ten dollars a year the telegraph company guaranteed to advise its subscribers of the approach of all ships the moment they were sighted from Coney Island. For another fee, when weather permitted, the company would accept messages to be telegraphed to Coney Island and put aboard incoming ships as they neared the harbour.

Business was good but Samuel wanted to expand, he wrote to James in St Louis suggesting that a telegraph company be set up there but James was short of funds and suffering from a badly wounded leg, having been involved in a duel over a woman. Duels were against the law at that time so he was also looking at ten days in prison. He asked his brother for a loan and Samuel sent him a hundred dollars with the recommendation that he avoid duelling in the future. Apparently the ten days in prison wasn't too hard for him because he later told his brother that the ladies brought him

161

flowers and dainties and the men brought him wines and good cigars.

Samuel now turned his attention towards Boston, where the layout of the harbour was suitable for his ship news telegraph service. Robinson in New York, seems to have suddenly realised that although he was doing well out of the business, Samuel was doing much better with his cable manufacturing business and demanded an enquiry, accusing Samuel of getting more than his fair share out of the business.

The other stockholders disagreed, however, and saw no dishonesty in the way Samuel was selling to a company in which he had an interest. Robinson, however, started litigation against Colt. His case came to nothing in the end but it dragged on for several years.

Samuel's father Christopher, was not faring so well back in Hartford and he was frequently on the verge of bankruptcy. Samuel helped his father out financially as much as he could and he began visiting Hartford on occasion.

Hartford society was pleased to welcome the Hartford boy who had made good. Mrs. Lydia H. Sigourney, Hartford's favourite poet, became Samuel's social sponsor. They had known each other from childhood, and with her help he re-established himself back into the society to which his mother had been born and from which his father had been dropped when he married Olive.

© Lydia Huntley Sigourney 1791-1865
American poet, she was commonly known as
"The Sweet Singer of Hartford"

At the same time, he dropped the Congregationalist faith of his father, that he had always disliked, and joined the Episcopalians, who more suited his personality. Samuel liked his religion with music and saw no reason why decent folk should distance themselves from song and dance.

Samuel received the same patronage from Major Caldwell as his father had done and as an eligible bachelor, who was making a name for himself in New York and Washington, he attracted the attention of many a young heiress.

He was determined not to marry until he had made his fortune, however, there was one young lady who did attract his attention. Miss Elizabeth Jarvis was the daughter of Reverend William Jarvis an Episcopalian rector at Middletown, Connecticut, and she was as attracted to Samuel as he was to her. Miss Jarvis was an understanding and apparently patient lady and it seems she was also prepared to wait until Samuel had achieved his ambition of making his fortune.

Elizabeth Colt, nee Jarvis   1826-1905

Elizabeth did not understand Samuel's inventions and could not visualise, as Samuel did, a country interconnected with telegraph wires on poles, over which messages could be sent in the blinking of an eye, but she had faith in Samuel and was willing to believe in his vision, although there were many who didn't.

All this while, trouble was brewing in Texas. It had been admitted into the Union in 1845, something that the Mexican government regarded as a theft of territory and they made it plain that, if the United States wanted Texas, they would have to fight for it. With Congress having admitted Texas to the Union, President Polk had no choice other than to protect it, to which end he sent General Taylor down to the Rio Grande.

The Mexicans warned Taylor to withdraw but it soon became apparent that he had no such intention and they began making preparations to drive him out. Mexican cavalry began patrolling the border and when Colonel Cross of the American army was discovered riding beyond the lines he was killed. When an American patrol under the leadership of Captain Thornton was sent out to search for Cross, they were ambushed by the Mexicans and only Thornton escaped, the rest being either killed or taken prisoner.

Thornton had been in Washington when Colt had been trying to interest the government in his revolver. He had been impressed with the gun and had done his best to persuade the Ordnance Bureau to adopt it. Although his efforts had been in vain, Samuel had presented Thornton with a pair of pistols as appreciation for his efforts and it was with these that he had fought his way to freedom from the Mexican ambush.

Thornton soon discovered that he was not the only one impressed by the weapon, and that many officers in his command were similarly armed. Captain Samuel Walker, whom Colt had met before and who had been guarding Thornton's lines of communication, declared that the only thing wrong with Colt's gun, was that fact that there were too few of them, and he urged that something be done to remedy the situation.

Walker was dispatched to Washington with orders to make the government aware of the army's needs and by this time, President Polk had an unpopular war on his hands and the States of Connecticut, New Jersey, Pennsylvania and New York, had made it plain that their Militia could not be counted on for service in far off Texas.

Recruiting for the regular army was proving difficult, what Polk needed was some way of enhancing the performance of the troops he already had at his disposal, so when Walker arrived with tales of Colt's wonderful revolver, it seemed like the perfect solution. Walker was authorised to get in touch with Colt and arrange for a supply of his guns.

Captain Samuel Walker 1817-1847
Texas Ranger

Samuel Colt was in Hartford visiting Miss Jarvis, having just come from Boston where he knew full well that sentiment was against the war. It mattered nothing to the residents of Boston or Hartford or the businesses of New York, whether Texas was a republic, a Mexican province or a state in the Union, and he could see no business in it, Mexico had no navy and Polk had no need of submarine mines.

When Samuel returned to his rooms at the Goris Hotel, Boston, however, he found a letter waiting for him from Captain Walker. The Texas Ranger was waiting for Samuel in Yew York and urged him to join him there without delay, he had urgent government business to discuss.

As soon as Samuel arrived, Walker asked, *"How soon can you let me have a thousand of your pistols?"*

"As soon as I can build a shop and make them," replied Samuel.

Colt explained to Walker that all the Machinery, patterns and models of the Patent Arms Manufacturing Company, had been sold at foreclosure in Paterson for $62,00. Samuel didn't even have a model of his own invention.

He declared that he would borrow one of Walker's pistol and make patterns from that, but Walker didn't have his pistols with him. The two men set out to purchase one but none could be found for sale. In the end, Samuel sat down and designed a new, improved arm and set out to find someone to make it.

Eventually he turned to Eli Whitney and signed a contract for the basic parts for his thousand pistols. These parts included barrels, cylinders and certain castings, the minor parts Samuel acquired elsewhere and he did his own assembling.

Walker got his thousand pistols in a remarkably short time, all things considered and Colt was given an order for an additional thousand. Eli Whitney realised that Samuels revolver had finally got the recognition it deserved and he was anxious to form some kind of partnership with Colt but Samuel would have none of it.

Whitney had a couple of lawyers look into Samuels patent rights, he thought maybe he could force Samuel into a partnership by buying up whatever interest the Paterson company may have held, but he was unsuccessful.

Samuel's friends told him of Whitney's activities and Samuel prepared to set up his own shop, much to Whitney's dismay. He tried to dissuade Samuel by pointing out that he couldn't hope to set up such a well-equipped plant as Whitney's with the limited capital at his disposal, but Samuel was having none of it. He told Whitney that he considered his plant little better than makeshift and that the cost of production was far too high, he even said that the product, when delivered, barely passed inspection. Samuel was also aggrieved because he was of the opinion that Whitney had taken advantage of Samuel's position and charged him an outrageous price.

Eli Whitney knew that the government was paying Samuel $28 for each gun and he suspected that this gave Samuel a profit of $10 on every pistol, whereas he had to be content with a profit of a few hundred dollars on the entire contract. Whitney developed an intense dislike for Samuel Colt and whenever he could, he tried his best to turn opinion against him.

Both men had their allies in high places and Whitney supporters claimed that Colt's guns were too expensive and that the waste of federal money should stop. They managed to get the Senate to pass a resolution asking for information on the entire Colt business.

In April 1848 President Polk sent a brief message along with a report by the Secretary of War.

To the Senate of the United States:

In answer to the resolution of the Senate of the 28th March 1848, I communicate herewith a report of the Secretary of War, transmitting a report of the head of the Ordnance Bureau, with the accompanying papers relative to the firearms invented by Samuel Colt. Such is the favourable opinion entertained of the value of this arm, particularly for a mounted corps, that the Secretary of War, as will be seen by his report, has contracted with Mr. Colt for two thousand of his pistols. He has offered to contract for an additional number at liberal prices, but the inventor is unwilling to furnish them at the prices named in his offer.

The invention for the construction of these arms being patented, the United States cannot manufacture them at the government armouries without a previous purchase of the right to do so. The right to use this patent by the United States the inventor is unwilling to dispose of at a price deemed reasonable.

James K. Polk

Samuel decided that if he was to set up his own factory then he would do it in Hartford, so he rented space in a three-story building on Pearl Street, set up his machinery and was producing guns by the spring of 1848.

Samuel made enquiries to discover who was stirring up trouble for him and was not surprised discover that it was a friend of Whitney, Colonel George Talcott.

In order to counteract the influence that the Talcott-Whitney alliance was having, Samuel had several pairs of elaborately engraved and superbly finished presentation pistols made and he presented them where he thought they would do the most good.

General David Twiggs, Colonel Jack Hays of the Texas Rangers and Ben McCulloch, were among the beneficiaries of Samuel's generosity and when they wrote to thank him, he asked them to share they praises with Congress and the President, and most obliged him.

Whitney's opportunity to put the oar in came when Samuel sold the government a quantity of accessories without first obtaining a contract. He sent the government a bill for $3,000, which was cut to $1,500 by the House of Representatives on the advice of Talcott. Colt protested but was forced to except the reduced amount, commenting that if the government could not afford to pay him for his merchandise he would,

"Make a gift of the $1,500 out of which I regard myself as cheated."

Soon afterwards, Samuel offered to make ten thousand revolvers for $25 each and said that if he received a definite order for one hundred thousand, he would reduce the price even more. His critics quickly jumped on this and pointed out that if he could produce pistols for $25, how could he possibly argue that $28 was a fair price?

Samuel Colt was one of only a few individuals at that time to appreciate the economy that could be made by mass production and he was one of the first to apply mass production methods to standardized parts, but Samuel was not about to share his wisdom with Congress.

Samuel was also quick to realise that the constant discussion about his invention was good publicity and his name and his product was soon known around the world.

Chapter Eleven

Success at Last

Small orders for Colt's revolver, but orders nevertheless, began to arrive from England, France, Russia and Turkey and they were promptly filled. At first the guns were stamped "Col. Colt. New York" but that was soon altered to "Col. Sam'l Colt, Hartford."

Samuel Colt was no longer reliant on government handouts to run his business and he had a new air of authority about him, he could now go to Washington and say, "These are my guns, this is my price, take it or leave it."

Many said that this attitude was ungrateful after all the help he had received but Colt pointed out that it was the government that had come to him, and that he had forfeited his profitable telegraph business to aid the war effort. If the government had accepted his guns before the Paterson plant had been forced to close, he could have supplied the army at the very start of the Mexican War.

The Mexican War had not just promoted Colt and his guns around the world, it had broken the Spanish stronghold on a large part of the West and Southwest.

A vast number of land seekers were now heading into unmapped areas that were previously the sole domain of Indians and buffalo. Gold was discovered in California, calling fortune hunters and adventurers to the Pacific Coast and the lands through which these people had to pass were full of hostile Indian tribes, as well as outcasts and desperadoes.

The wise among those who travelled this dangerous path considered it better to do so with decent protection. A reliable arm, even if was an expensive item, was considered a worthwhile expenditure, even if it meant going short on some rations, and the revolver was the weapon of choice.

Unlike the American government, Colt had an eye for what was happening abroad, war clouds were looming over Europe and Samuel contacted the heads of all the governments to let them know that his arms were available to them, should they wish to purchase.

While Whitney and his followers were still doing what they could to bring Colt down, Samuel was expanding his Hartford factory, and installing more machinery, he was getting ever closer to his dream of having every part of every revolver of a similar calibre and design, completely interchangeable.

It wasn't long before the Hartford factory was becoming too small, especially when Samuel appointed David

K. Torrey as his Mexican agent, not that the Mexicans needed any convincing of the worth of Colt's gun, having been on the receiving end of it during the Mexican War, and it wasn't long before every Mexican who could scrape together the cost of a revolver was armed with one.

Samuel's enemies were still at work and a certain, Leavett, produced a revolver that was a slight refinement of Colt's product and a clear infringement of his patent. This didn't bother Samuel's enemies. They assumed that Colt's patent would expire in 1853 and that by the time any suit for infringement could be concluded there would no longer be a case.

What they didn't know and hadn't bothered to find out, was that Colt had applied for and obtained an extension of his patent.

In 1849 the Massachusetts Arms Company began manufacturing revolvers of the Leavett design, at Chicopee Falls. Samuel suspected and always maintained that Whitney was backing the company.

Samuel waited until the plant was in production before bringing a suit and demanding a royalty be paid for every arm manufactured to date and that production be stopped.

Colt's interests were represented by Edward N. Dickerson, a leading attorney. The Massachusetts Arms

Company employed Samuel Rufus Choate, who realised that if Colt's patent stood up, then his clients would lose, so he dug back in time. He showed the court examples of earlier repeating arms with a rotating cylinder and a single barrel including that of one James Puckle of London in 1718. He claimed that the existence of such weapons discredited Colt's claim to have invented the revolver principle.

Dickerson countered the argument by having a model of Puckle's gun brought into court and placed alongside one of Colt's guns. Puckle's weapon was mounted on a tripod base and needed two people to carry it. Colt's claim was upheld and the Massachusetts company stopped trading.

A drawing of Puckle's gun patented in 1718

Colt travelled to Turkey and obtained an audience with the Sultan, to whom he presented a pair of beautifully finished and engraved revolvers and the Sultan was appreciative enough of the gift to give Samuel a magnificent jewelled snuff-box in return. During his meeting with the Sultan, Samuel carelessly let slip that he had heard that the Russians were equipping their forces with revolvers. The Sultan, was of course grateful for the apparent indiscretion and decided it would be prudent to place an order for five thousand of Colt's pistols, to be delivered at the earliest possible date.

Samuel, it seems, had forgotten to mention that the Russians were buying the guns from Colt himself, mainly because he had mentioned to them that the Turks were buying revolvers.

Returning to Hartford with huge orders he recognised at once that the Pearl Street factory was too small and he took over a large disused cotton mill, but only as a stop-gap.

He started looking for a site that would be big enough for unlimited expansion and one where he could bring in the raw materials by steamship and load his merchandise directly onto ships for delivery.

London beckons

Colt came to England in 1851, not just to exhibit his guns at the Great Exhibition at Crystal Palace, but also to look for a suitable site for a European factory. At the Exhibition, his gun met with almost universal acclaim, not so much because of the mechanism itself, but because of the robust character of the weapon and the method of manufacture.

Colt gave a lecture on his improved mass-production methods to the Institute of Civil Engineering in 1851. A lecture for which he received the "Telford" gold medal.

A Telford Gold Medal similar to the one received by Samuel Colt

The London factory operated between 1853 and 1857 and was run on the same lines as his American operations. The bulk of his staff recruited in London were unskilled or semiskilled workers but the foremen and key workers were men who had trained at his factory in Hartford.

Colt's London factory was basically independent of the established English gun trade and it was capable of turning out extremely reliable arms at a price that made competition difficult. This was not easy for the established trade to accept and there followed a great deal of criticism and abuse. There were accusations of shoddy workmanship and sharp practices at the factory and there were personal attacks upon Colt himself.

Any real examination of the guns produced at the factory at that time however, would have given the lie to the claims, and in fact, no lesser person than Charles Dickens, who visited the factory in 1854, and was fully aware of the sort of conditions that existed in such places, declared himself to have been most favourably impressed by the smooth and efficient working of the whole system, the neat finish of the arms and the excellent working conditions and high wages of the operatives.

Dickens also states that the output of the factory was 600 finished arms per week and at the time of his visit, the storeroom was empty because demand was obviously far outstripping supply.

The list price for a standard Navy Colt in England, together with a bullet-mould casting both round and conical bullets, a cleaning rod and a combined turn-screw and nipple-key was £5–10–0.   The price of the pocket revolver was £4-0–0 with the same accessories. Plain wooden boxes or holsters could be purchased as extras and prices could be supplied for specially engraved presentation pieces in mahogany or rosewood cases.

It was during a visit to his London establishment that Samuel Colt had the audacity to claim that, he could manufacture muskets at a lower price and of better quality, by machine, than could be done by Her Majesty's Armouries!

With the start of the Crimean war only months away Colt found himself called before a House of Commons committee, who were very much opposed to both his plans and his methods.

After a hand-made Minié rifle was handed to him, he was asked, *"Do you consider that muskets manufactured by machinery in America are as well fabricated as the Minié rifle which has been submitted to you?"*

Samuel examined the arm with care before replying, *"There is none so badly made at our national armouries as the*

Minié rifle shown me. That arm would not pass one of our inspectors."

It may be of interest to some if I explain something of the Minié rifle Colt was shown, and I have included this as an appendix at the end of the book, for those who wish to read it.

The enquiry switched tack and turned their attention to the reasons that Colt had established a business in England. Was it not true that he was trying to grab the government business in the event of war, with his offers of quantity production at low prices? Had he not written and offered terms by which he would supply muskets to the Ordnance?

Samuel admitted that he had written to the Ordnance and that he had said that, for the outlay of £100.000 on machinery, plant and accessories, he could supply one million muskets at thirty shillings a musket. These he pointed out, would have the advantage of uniformity and interchangeability, and none that are so made will be inferior to the best that can now be found in Her Majesty's service for military purposes.

Lord Seymour presiding, turned the inquiry back to machine production. He was unable to understand how a machine could possibly turn out work as good as that of a master gunsmith.

Samuel explained, *"I do not say that they can make a single arm as well as well as a master artisan, but if you give one hundred arms to an American inspector, made at any place you choose by contract in England, more would be condemned out of them, even if made expressly, than if you took the arms made by machinery. If you give a machinist a model, he will make them all alike. If you give that man a bad model, they will all be bad. The secret of good machine production is having the model for which the machine is set, of the desired quality."*

Further questioning by the committee showed that they had not grasped the theory of quantity production, they could not understand why, if a million muskets could be produced by machinery at a certain price per musket, a lesser number could not be turned out at the same cost per gun.

Samuel explained, *"One does not figure production costs on the bases of a single gun, or a single order, in terms of labour and materials. Machinery can be expected to last about ten years; so one tenth of the cost of that machine must be absorbed by its output each year and must be counted a production cost, whether you make one gun or one million. Add to that your material and labour costs, your taxes and incidental expenses and a reasonable profit. Divide the total by the number of guns you have produced and that gives you your selling price."*

The committee continued to quiz Colt, now turning their attention to his sales in America and he was asked, *"What is the price at which you have supplied those arms to the government?"*

"I supply them for anything I can get." Colt replied.

"What have you supplied them to the government for?"

"I do not choose to tell you. The government will answer the question for themselves. I will tell nobody what I supply my arms for. If you want to buy, and say you will buy ten thousand of them, and will give me a fair price, you can have them today."

Samuel must have found the whole thing very frustrating, because of course, the only thing that really interested him was selling his revolver not muskets.

The main rival to Colt's revolver in Britain was the Deane-Adams revolver. A five-chamber double action pistol, (double action because pulling the trigger, both cocked and fired the gun, whereas Colt's pistols were all single action, they had to be cocked manually first before firing.) It also differed from Colt's revolvers in being of solid frame construction, that is to say, one in which both the barrel and the frame of the pistol were shaped in a single forging, whereas Colt's pistols had the barrels made separately.

Although the parts of the Deane-Adams were not as interchangeable as the Colt models, it was a mass-produced weapon and was manufactured in large quantities at the Deane-Adams factory in Southwark and by various contractors in Birmingham, England and Liege in Belgium.

As might have be expected, there was great rivalry between Colt and Adams and it was bitter rivalry rather than friendly. Supporters of Colt were adamant that a double-action or "self-cocking" revolver was totally unsound and could have no value, an opinion that might well have been based on the self-cocking pepper-box and transition revolvers that preceded the Adams.

In truth, both makes had their advantages and disadvantages. Colt had an advantage in range and accuracy which made it a better weapon in skirmishes, whilst the Adams revolver was better suited to close hand-to-hand fighting in which hard hitting and quick shooting was of more value.

The rivalry between Adams and Colt and their struggle to promote their guns as the better arm, took on more importance when the British War Office began to recognise the importance of the revolver as a military arm.

During the Spring of 1854, a committee, appointed by the War Office, tested both the Colt and the Adams pistols at Woolwich. Although the tests were not conclusive, the Board of Ordnance, without officially adopting it as a service arm, purchased as many as 40,000 pistols of Colt's Navy model between 1854 and 1856.

Despite the large order it would seem that the higher military authorities were still unconvinced of the revolvers value as a military weapon. Even though Britain was engaged in a Continental war at the time of purchase, no new weapons were issued to troops bound for the Crimea and only a small number were supplied to the Navy for the use of officers.

Evan at the time of the Indian Mutiny, when thousands of revolvers were in store, only very few were issued. Officers on the front line however, unlike their superiors, appreciated the revolver's value and in both the Crimean and Indian campaigns, officers purchased their own and the revolver was in general use.

It is interesting to note that in the Crimea, the favoured weapon was the Colt, but during the Indian campaign, just three years later, it was the Adams that was the favoured pistol. A circumstance due in part to the experience gained in actual warfare, and in part to improvements made to the Adams pistol between 1854 and 1857.

The case for the Adams revolver was highlighted by two reported incidents, first from the Crimea when J. G. Crosse of the 88th Regiment wrote to Adams:

"I had one of the largest-sized revolver pistols at the bloody battle of Inkermann and by some chance got surrounded by Russians. I then found the advantages of your pistol over that of Colonel Colt's, for had I to cock before each shot, I should have lost my life. I should not have had time to cock, as they were too close to me, being only a few yards from me; so close that I was bayonetted through the thigh immediately after shooting the fourth man."

Speaking of the Sepoy Mutiny in India, Lieutenant Colonel G. V. Fosbury reported:

"An officer, who especially prided himself on his pistol shooting, was attacked by a stalwart mutineer armed with a heavy sword. The officer, unfortunately for himself, carried a Colt's Navy pistol, which, as you may remember, was of small calibre, .36, and fired a sharp-pointed picket bullet of sixty to the pound and a heavy charge of powder, its range being at least 600 yards, as I have frequently proved. This he proceeded to empty into the sepoy as he advanced, but having done so, he waited just one second too long to see the effect of his shooting and was cloven to the teeth by his antagonist, who then dropped down and died beside him. My informant, who witnessed the

affair, told me that five out of the six bullets had struck the sepoy close together in the chest and had all passed through him and out at his back."

The adoption of the Adams revolver as the standard service revolver of the British Army marked the end of the great Adams-Colt controversy of the early fifties and destroyed any hopes that Colt may have had of securing any further large contracts from the British Government.

It cannot be a coincidence that the Organisation of The London Armoury Company for the production of the improved double action Adams revolver, coincided with Colt's decision to close down his London factory in 1856.

Colt's London factory on the Thames 1853

Although Colt closed his London factory, his revolvers remained popular and they continued to sell well in Britain and in the rest of Europe. In fact, almost every serious power was purchasing some of Colt's pistols and the armoury in Hartford was continually having to expand and increase its production, something that was beginning to put a strain on the general manager, Milton Joslin.

A plant superintendent was needed and Samuel remembered a young mechanic whom he had met years ago in Ware. Elisha K. Root was working as general superintendent at the Collins Company plant in Collinsville, Connecticut, where tools and general hardware were being produced. Root had invented a number of ways of reducing manufacturing costs and Samuel decided he was just the man for the job.

Samuel, in characteristic style, wrote to Root, telling him that he had a position for him as *"superintendent of my armoury, and would like to know how soon you could report for work. I will pay as much as you are now receiving, and if that is not satisfactory you may yourself fix such compensation as you think fair and reasonable. The important thing is that you come to me at the earliest possible moment."*

When Root started work for Colt, he justified Samuel's faith in him almost immediately by improving existing machines and inventing several new devices that cut costs and increased production. In fact, Root managed to improve things so much that pistols were selling for half of what the old Paterson model cost.

Elisha K. Root

Orders were still coming in faster than they could be filled, however and more expansion was needed. Samuel's vision now was to be able to load orders directly onto ships from his factory.

Chapter Twelve

Armsmear

Samuel purchased several parcels of land in Hartford, in what was known as South Meadow and eventually acquired some five hundred acres that reached all the way down to the banks of the Connecticut River. From there he could load directly onto ships to carry his arms all over the world.

Map of Hartford 1640
Showing South Meadow

His purchases aroused some mirth amongst the inhabitants of Hartford however, who supposed he must have forgotten, from his childhood there, that almost every spring the river was in full flood, and at least half of South Meadow was under water. Some years when the snow melted up north the river could rise enough for water to reach even the city of Hartford itself.

Samuel hadn't been forgetful however, what he had been, was to Holland. If the Dutch could keep the ocean off their land by building dykes, then Samuel Colt could keep the Connecticut River off his land in the same way.

As soon as he had acquired the land, he began building a dyke approximately two miles long. He knew that the river had reached heights of over twenty-seven feet and ordered the dyke be built high enough to keep the land safe if it happened again.

As it happens, one year during the five-year construction of the dyke, the river rose to a record height and Samuel had to order the height of the dyke be increased to thirty-three feet, some four feet higher than the record flood.

There was much criticism in the local papers of Samuel's efforts and many stated that he was doomed to failure.

One man, calling himself "Taxpayer" wrote to the paper saying that trying to keep the river off South Meadow by building embankments was like closing the hatches on a sinking ship with the bottom holed. Some even suggested that he had lost his reason and should be declared insane.

The editor himself replied to the correspondent, writing, *"It may be true enough that the work proposed by Col. Colt is difficult of accomplishment, but he is a practical man, and is willing and able to take the risk; and in place of grumbling about his project, we ought to allow him to take the risk, and the benefits of the risk, if there be any in it.*

Samuel ignored all the criticism at first but when it persisted, he decided to reply in kind. He had never been a man to pay his taxes willingly, so when he replied in the paper he wrote declaring,

"it is not very generous in "Taxpayer" to take an opportunity for attacking me when all my attention is required to protect my property from the destructive flood which is upon us; but I am not yet discouraged, even by the combined forces of the land and water. The floods have lifted up their heads' higher than ever before; but that only proves the greater necessity of protection against them. Every year a scene like that of today is enacted, but we do nothing to guard property and life; and when any one citizen is willing to incur the risk of

contending with the river, such people as the "Tax payer" do all they can to defeat him.

Now sir I am not afraid to face the music or create it; and if the City of Hartford will agree to relieve my property from increased taxation I will bind myself to exclude the river from the South Meadows, and more than that, I will agree to dyke the Connecticut River from end to end of the city, so that nothing less than Noah's flood can reach the houses which are now inundated.

The circulation of the river in this city is not such a blessing that we ought to incur these heavy losses every spring to enjoy it."

One clergyman announced in the paper, that the record flood was a punishment sent from God for Samuel seeking to control the forces of nature.

It is worth noting that on 27th December 1855, the Council was authorised by the city voters, following Samuel Colt's example, to construct a dyke along the northern bank of Little River and the western bank of the Connecticut river, so as to protect the portion of the city that was annually flooded.

When all the land Colt required was purchased, he set about building his armoury, and on the land's highest point facing Wethersfield Road and well above the high-water mark was a gentle slope where Colt intended to build his manor house, "Armsmear."

Armsmear was completed early in 1857 and was largely modelled on the Italian villas Samuel had visited on his extensive European tours.

The house was furnished in the most opulent manner with fine furniture paintings and sculptures, all to show any visitors to his home, just how far Samuel Colt had come.

One magazine described the house as *"long, grand, impressive, contradictory, beautiful and strange. It is a little Turkish among other things, with domes, pinnacles and light lavish ornamentation, yet...the feeling is English."*

Armsmear

Colt didn't stop at just building a spectacular house at Armsmear and filling it with works of art and souvenirs from his many travels, he also made sure that the grounds were just as impressive. There was a large lake, partially artificial, but filled by natural springs. The lake was filled with Chinese Carp that were clearly visible because of the clarity of the water, and the size of the lake was such that a rowing boat was often to be seen on it amongst the many swans.

Armsmear.—In the Grounds.

One corner of the lake at Armsmear

The Armoury

His armoury was also designed to impress the visitor and sported a large onion-shaped dome on its roof, painted with gold stars like the Russian and Arab palaces he had seen on his travels, and surmounted by the ubiquitous Colt Stallion.

Colt's armoury at Armsmear from across the river

The dome could be seen from most places in the city, and for miles if one was travelling on the river. Atop the onion dome was an unmistakable symbol of the man who'd had it constructed, a rampant colt stallion, rearing up on its hind legs.

The rampant colt stallion on top of the onion dome

The work at Colt's factory was split into small tasks, each performed by a different worker and to such an extent that the inside of a gun-stock was oiled by a different man from the one who oiled the outside. The thinking behind this division of labour was that even if you are talking about a task that can be taught to anyone in just a minute, a man who has been performing the task all day for several days will perform it maybe ten times in a minute, whereas a man who is new to the task will only achieve three or four in the same time.

Some tasks require more skill and training than others and the men who perform these tasks will be paid more money per hour of labour. If you give that man two tasks to perform one will likely be harder or more skilled than the other, so it makes no economic sense to pay him a higher wage for performing both, when the simpler task could be done by a man on a lower wage.

Adam Smith said, *"- division of labour saves much time that would be lost, were workmen to change from one kind of work to another. He who now performs three thousand manipulations on a single tool, how many would he bring to pass if he undertook to work upon three thousand tools a day?*

As stated in, John Stuart Mill's Political Economy, *"- as springing from divided labours, is the less amount of wages with which the same end may be compassed. If I hire a single man to complete with his own hands an entire gun, I must pay for all the time consumed in constructing it, and so for the simplest processes, the price of very accomplished handicraftsman; this is taking a beetle to kill a fly, or climbing over the house to open the gate. Mark the contrast when that arm is made not by one, but by one hundred and fifty-four operatives. No longer need we "cut blocks with a razor." The experts are now better off than any of their class of old, for they earn five dollars a day; while boys, just beginning on the most facile parts of the milling, are content with a tithe of that sum. Besides, those boys are roused to do their best, knowing that* all experts were once boys, and hoping to become experts themselves.

We may perhaps add, as a fifth advantage of dividing labour, that it opens a door of occupation to all. If all members in the body politic have not the same office, yet all members have an office, and that the one best suited to them. The hand cannot say to the foot. "I have no need of thee." One man is too ignorant to manage a machine for stocking, but he can oil that machine, or at least sweep away its chips, a service for which two men are paid each a dollar a day. Here then are shallows where a lamb my ford, and depths where the elephant must swim.

"Solomon, seeing the young Jeroboam, that he was industrious, made him a ruler." So, few contractors but were wise enough, if an underling shows pluck and grit, to try him with a task harder, higher and more suited to develop him. Thus, in a single month, he grows skilled in milling; in three months more, in drilling; in a year he can make his own drills; and with study, industry and brans, after four years longer – just the college curriculum – he may finish an education truly liberal, and graduate as a master modeller. Thus, is this republic of arts, division of labour.

It is difficult to imagine what it must have been like inside Samuel Colt's factory but we do have some help, firstly with an extract from,

"Armsmear, The Home, The Arm, And The Armoury Of Samuel Colt. A Memorial."

The gyrations, many of them, concerning stubborn materials, or delicate processes, no result are apparent to a transient observer, but the universal whirl seems as aimless as the spinning of a top, or the spouting of a fountain. Work of every kind looks like play to children. They never witness an execution without considering it a sort of joke, and so for weeks afterwards they play Jack Ketch. To them the mystery of pistol-making is only a line in Mother Goose: "here we go round, round, roundly." All outsiders, in their views of mechanical mysteries, are only children of a larger growth.

They look on the processes as hastened, like a juggler's sleight of hand, on purpose to dodge their detecting the secret. Or, they misunderstand their nature as much as one of our statesmen, on his visit to Rome, did that of the Vatican frescoes, when he mistook them for a series of Dan Rices's circus show-bills. But what is in brief the aim of these whirligigs, of this giddy circling, and of the movements, rectilinear or eccentric, into which it is often converted? It is simply to render a few bits of wood, iron, steel and copper, rough or smooth, hollow or solid, manifold in size, shape and colour; to harmonize them by mutual adaptations, so that they can be compacted as members in one whole body; to produce facsimiles of these patterns outnumbering the myriads in any army, and that in the least time, and at the least cost; as well as prove, in defiance of all cavils, that these tasks have been smoothly done. This is the purpose of the armoury.

How is this purpose accomplished? By thousands of steam-driven machines, which are costly, and whose operations, while seeming slow or roundabout, really attain the ends in view more swiftly, perfectly, and in instances more oft-repeated, than were otherwise possible. Many of these contrivances were invented on the spot. All of them are claimed as American in origin, so that had the geologist Lyell beheld them, he must have pronounced that they, and not Common Schools, were "the most original product of American mind."

Secondly, if that rather flowery description is difficult to follow, we fortunately have a contemporary account of a visit to the factory that still exists.

A Day at the Armory of Colt's Patent Fire-Arms Manufacturing Company," United States Magazine, vol. 4, no. 3 (March 1857): 221-249.

"The motive power is located about in the centre of the main building. It consists of a steam engine—cylinder, 36 inches in diameter, 7 foot stroke, fly-wheel 30 feet in diameter, weighing 7 tons. This engine, which is rated at 250 horse power, is supplied with the well-known "Sickel's Cutoff," (see appendix) which the superintendent and engineer speak of as the most useful and important addition to the steam-engine since the days of Watt.

The steam is furnished from two cylindrical boilers, each 22 feet long and 7 feet in diameter. The power is carried to the attic by a belt working on the fly-wheel; this belt is 118 feet long by 22 inches wide, and travels at the rate of 2,500 feet per minute.

Fully appreciating the great interest manifested by our readers in descriptions of this kind, we will now proceed to conduct them through the interior of this immense industrial pile, and on the way we will endeavour to explain, as understandingly as possible, the various processes of the manufacture, from the raw metal and wood, to the complete and effective arms familiarly known as Colt's Revolvers.

Leaving the office we cross the bridge, pass down through the machine shop, engine room, etc., to the rear parallel, an apartment 40 by 50 feet square, the centre of which is appropriated as the store-room for iron and steel. Large quantities of these materials, in bars and rods, are stored here in charge of a responsible party, whose duty it is to fill the orders from the contractors, and render an accurate statement of such deliveries to the main storekeeper's department. This latter system is universal throughout the establishment—thus the materials of all kinds can be readily accounted for, no matter what their state of transposition.

The furnaces and anvils of Colt's forging shop.
From United States Magazine, 1857.

We now follow them to the armoury proper, which, in the first place, is the second storey of the front parallel. This is probably not only the most spacious, but the best arranged and fitted workshop extant. We fully understand this to be a broad and sweeping assertion, yet we have an abundance of competent authority to back the opinion. On first entering this immense room, from the office, the tout ensemble is really grand and imposing, and the beholder is readily impressed with an exalted opinion of the vast mechanical resources of the corporation.

The room is 500 feet long by 60 feet wide, and 16 feet high. It is lighted, on all sides, by 110 windows that reach nearly from floor to ceiling; it is warmed by steam from the boilers—the pipers being under the benches, running completely around the sides and ends; there are the perfect arrangements for ventilation, and sufficient gas burners to illuminate the whole for night-work.

Running along through the centre is a row of cast-iron columns, sixty in number, to which is attached the shafting—which here is arranged as a continuous pulley—for driving the machines, as close together as possible, only allowing sufficient space to get around and work them. The whole of this immense floor space is covered with machine tools. Each portion of the fire-arm has its particular section.

As we enter the door the first group of machines appears to be exclusively employed in chambering cylinders; the next turning and shaping them; here another is boring barrels; another group is milling the lock frames; still another is drilling them; beyond are a score of machines boring and screw-cutting the nipples, and next to them a number of others are making screws; here are the rifling machines, and there the machines for boring rifle-barrels; now we come to the jigging machines that mortice out the lock-frames; and thus it goes on all over this great hive of physical and mental exertion.

The second floor of Colt's East Armory, showing dozens of machine tools and operators, powered by overhead pulley, belts, and shafting. From United States Magazine, 1857.

As soon as completed the different parts are carried to the storey above, which, with the exception of the machinery and the columns through the centre, is an exact counterpart of the room below. It is designated the Inspecting and Assembling Department. Here the different parts are most minutely inspected; this embraces a series of operations which in the aggregate amount to considerable; the tools to inspect a cylinder, for example, are fifteen in number, each of which must gauge to a hair; the greatest nicety is observed, and it is absolutely impossible to get a slighted piece of work beyond this point.

The finished arm is laid on a rack, ready for the prover; of course, many others accompany it to the department of this official, which is located in the third story of the rear building. Here each chamber is loaded with the largest charge possible, and practically tested by firing; after which, they are wiped out by the prover and returned to the inspection department. The inspectors again take them apart, thoroughly clean and oil them, when they are for the last time put together and placed in a rack for the final inspection. This is done by Mr. William Tuller, a gentleman who has been in the constant employment of Colonel Colt since the manufacture commenced in Hartford.

The parts having been so thoroughly examined and tested, it would seem that this last inspection was scarcely necessary; but, after a short observation, we saw several laid aside. Taking up one with a small mark on the barrel, "Why do you reject this?" we inquired. "Pass that to-day, and probably much larger blemishes would appear tomorrow," replied Mr. T. The order from the Principal is perfection; and a small scratch in the bluing or varnish is sufficient to prevent the arm passing. The finished arm is now returned to the store room; from whence, after being papered, they are sent to the wareroom—situated in the basement of the office building; from this they are sent to nearly every portion of the habitable globe.

In round numbers it might be stated that supposing the cost of an arm to be 100; of this the wages of those who attended to and passed pieces through the machines was 10 per cent, and those of the best class workmen engaged in assembling the weapons was also 10 per cent, thus leaving 80 per cent for the duty done by the machinery.

With the exception of the steam engine and boilers, a majority of the machinery was not only invented, but constructed on the premises. When this department was commenced, it was the intention of the Company to manufacture solely for their own use. Some months since, applications were made by several foreign Governments to be supplied with machines and the right to operate them. After mature deliberation, it was concluded to supply orders, and on the day of our visit we saw a complete set of machinery for manufacturing fire-arms, that will shortly be shipped to a distant land. The Company have now determined to incorporate this manufacture as a branch of their regular business. The machine shop is the lower floor of the front parallel; its dimensions are 60 by 500 feet; it is supplied with power and hand tools of every desired kind, all of the most approved construction.

One of Colt's workers at an unidentified machine

Another of the numerous inventions of Colonel Colt is the Metallic Foil Cartridge, a contrivance that always insures "dry powder' to the possessor. Tin foil, cut in the required shape, is formed in an inverted cone, which is charged with gunpowder; the ball is oval, with a flat end; a circle is pierced near the edge, on this flat end, to receive the edge of the foil; on the cone and ball being brought together, the joint is closed by pressure; they are then enclosed in paper wrappers, so arranged that this covering can be instantly removed when the cartridge is about to be used. The whole operation is completed so perfectly that the cartridge is entirely impervious to water, as by experiment they have repeatedly been fired after having been immersed for hours. Owing to the peculiar shape of the bore of the nipple in Colt's firearms, the fire from the percussion caps readily penetrated the foil, without pricking.

They are manufactured in a building erected expressly for the purpose, situated about half a mile south of the armoury. No fire is allowed in any part of the works, heat being furnished by steam generated in an out-building. Nearly the whole labour here is performed by females, about thirty of whom were at work during our visit—the foreman, engineer and charger making the complement of employees.

Women at work in Colt's factory

The principal officers of the company consist of, Colonel Colt as President; E. K. Root, Esq., Superintendent, and Luther P. Sargeant, Esq., Treasurer and Secretary; besides these, there is a chief to each department—Mr. Horace Lord being master workman in the armoury.

Colonel Colt has been particularly fortunate in the selection of his immediate associates; they are all men of mark. Mr. Root, to whom we are indebted for a few hours of valuable instruction, is one of the most accomplished, practical and scientific mechanics of the day; although only in the prime of life, he has established a most enviable position, and his opinions on mooted questions of mechanism are eagerly sought after, even by the principals of some of our most extensive city establishments. Colonel Colt informed us that since their first connection all his views had been most ably seconded and put in practical operation by Mr. Root. In fact, the whole manufacture of every description is under his immediate direction.

Although so much care and attention have been exercised in perfecting the armoury, its accessories and products, yet the general welfare of the employees has not been neglected; most extensive arrangements for their comfort and convenience are in the course of rapid completion. And we may here remark that they are deserving of such especial favour; as *a body they are mostly young men, many of them having commenced their business life in the establishment. It was, in a measure, necessary to educate men expressly for the purpose, as the manipulation required is not exclusively that of the gunsmith, or of the machinist, but a combination of both of these callings. Taken as a whole, we found them decidedly a reading and thinking community, and we venture the assertion, that it would be difficult to produce a counterpart of mental capacity in the same number of mechanics employed in a manufactory. That they are well compensated for their services is evinced from the fact of the pay-roll amounting to from $1,000 to $1,200 per day.*

The grounds around the armoury have been laid out in squares of 500 feet each by streets 60 feet wide; upon these squares are being erected commodious three-story dwellings. Sufficient for about eighty families have already been finished, and are occupied by the employees; the operations will be continued until all who desire are accommodated. These houses have all the conveniences of city life. Gas works, of sufficient capacity to supply as large a population as can occupy the area, have already been erected and put in operation. Attached to the engine in the main building is a "cam pump," which raises the water from the Connecticut to a

reservoir on the hill beyond, from which it is distributed, by
pipes, to the armoury, dwellings, etc."

Footnote:

Extract from, "Armsmear, The Home, The Arm, And The
Armoury Of Samuel Colt. A Memorial."

"The stock wrought up in the arms factory, iron, steel.
Tin and the files are imported direct from England, and that in
a great degree, from the firm of Thomas Firth and Sons,
Sheffield. To be sure, as much steel is now made in the United
States as in any five European establishments, and the
American ores, above all, those on Lake Champlain are
regarded as no whit inferior to any in the world.

Notwithstanding, the arms company, though not
unpatriotic, and in spite of a thirty per cent duty, and high
exchange, cease not to depend altogether on England for raw
materials. Why is this? Simply, because the English smelt ores,
and turn iron to steel, by methods which result in a more
homogeneous staple than ours, so that weapons made of it less
often fail, when proved and inspected. The truth is, that in
fabricating steel, and its mother iron, young America has made
more haste than good speed. Forgetting the time-tried maxim,
"Make haste slowly, (Festina lente,) he has omitted some

laggard process as superfluous. Hence, he has fared like the stupid man who, in reporting an anecdote, fearing it will be tedious, brings it to you "just breaking off the point of it, and leaving out the pun." His iron is partly strong and partly broken, like the feet of Nebuchadnezzar's image, which stood tottering, their iron being mixed with miry clay.

It is an old Spanish dogma, that no iron is half so good for gun-barrels as that of old nails, which driven into the shoes of horses and mules, have been dashed against many a stone. But we can scarcely believe there is any magic in this particular mode of pounding, so haphazard and long drawn out, unless we believe, with Dr. Boyle, that the thigh-bone of a man wo has hung on the gallows is better as a medicine than any other.

All the force that is applied to horse-nails and making them, and through the kicks of brutes, may clearly be concentrated upon them in a few trip-hammer blows, "turning the accomplishment of many years into an hour-glass."

The real secret of securing good stock is now said to be this. Owing to the law of gravity, an unequal exposure to blast, when as susceptible to impression as a photographic negative, the lower part of the bar differs in texture from the upper. Let then each piece of iron and afterwards of blasted steel, be broken, and from the fragments let experts, even at this early stage, cull out those nodules which are best adapted for each variety of manufacture. One quality is best for tools, another for arms. Iron-workers can afford to pay more for stock in proportions as it better befits their several specialities.

They are confident their handiwork will not fail when put to the proof, if they can secure raw material which suits their needs as exactly as a square man fits a square corner, or as Lincoln's pegs fitted the holes when he sent Butler to New Orleans, and Grant to Vicksburg. Gun-makers agree with theologians, that the original sin is the mother of all others.

Let us follow a bit of raw material on its pilgrimage. If it be gun-metal, that is, copper alloyed unused with about ten per cent, of tin, its race is comparatively short. Going into the foundry, it is cast into pistol-guards and back straps. The moulds are so made that each turns out a dozen guards at once, the molten metal flowing into a sort of tree, with guards as branches. These, when cut off, milled, filed, and polished, pass to the electroplater, from whose batteries and solutions they are received by the burnishers. These brighteners now consist of ten, one man and nine girls.

One visitor thought to compliment this band by addressing them as Apollo and the nine Muses. But the operatives, being unused to classical allusions, scolded at him for calling them names. For their toil on each pistol, the tariff is three and one-half cents. The females daily complete about thirty sets—the man twice as many. The transformation from dull white to silvery lustre, by dint of mere friction with a steel dipped in soap and water, is astonishing.

Whenever a bar of steel or iron leaves the store-room, it starts on a long journey. It is first heated and cut on an anvil, or with shears, where the cutting is done quicker and better, into pieces short enough for convenient working. Having been again heated, it is, all in a moment, like so much wax or dough, forced into any desired shape on swage-blocks, or anvils cut in patterns. They are thus forced by hammers which, first raised by a screw rotating continuously, are then made to drop by touching a spring. They are hence named "drops." To a non-mechanical eye they seem more properly stamps than hammers, because they finish their work all at one blow, a blow so decisive and ponderous that it recalls the single stroke in the duel between Michael and Satan:

"The noble stroke uplifted high,
Which might at once determine, and not need repeat,
As not of power at once."

The score of forges, drawn up in a double range, must be in sharp contrast to those of Shakespeare's day, or he would not have represented Hamlet, when confessing himself the chief of sinners, saying his "imaginations were as foul as Vulcan's smithy. "Here a lady might venture to walk, with no more exposure of her finery than on a promenade along the streets of Pittsburg. If we may speak in Homeric style, these are a cluster of forges where Vulcan, the very god of iron-work, even when most full of the spirit of Momus, could find nothing to censure in walking from end to end of the files.

The fates awaiting our bit of metal, as it wends its way among the forges, are more various than the possible developments of a thought in the brain of Burns, which might perchance turn out a song, perchance turn out a sermon. According as it is iron or steel, and goes to one forge or another, will it become mainspring or cone nipple, lock-plate or lever, bullet-mould or pistol-barrel. A pistol-barrel, when stamped by the first drop, has a rude resemblance to a small dumb-bell with flattened heads. The next drop compresses one of its heads into a cylinder as narrow as its neck, leaving the other to form the barrel-shank for admitting the base-pin and ramrod lever. An outsider could not guess what to call a pistol-barrel when first blocked out. It is a bear's cub without form or fashion, which must be licked into shape by many a tongue-stroke of its dam.

The forge department is the special pride of both shops. Its machinery, mainly invented and patented by E. K. Root, Esq.

the present head of the concern, is the most labour-saving, and hence dollar-saving, of all the cunning contrivances here at work. For this kind of labour there was formerly required, at each anvil, a foreman with a helper. Now the helper alone can do more than three times the work of both, and can do it better than lies in the power of any human hands. In blocking out the lock-frame, since it is the most intricate of all members, the superiorities and economies of machinery are most conspicuous.

The apparatus for welding gun-barrels has been introduced since the rebellion broke out. All the barrels previously made, being of steel, needed no welding. In the welding process, flat bars of iron, on passing through the first groove in the rolling-machine, are "crimped," that is, hollowed, into the shape of the capital letter U. Next, they become short and thick as window weights, but are hollow, and with a slit on one side from end to end. When at a white heat, a mandrill, or a sort of iron foil, with a guard to screen the workman's hand, is thrust through them, and they are rolled through an eccentric groove between iron wheels, and this squeezing is repeated a dozen times. Each time they are spitted on a thinner foil, and are rolled through a narrower groove.

At the close, the side-splitting wounds have healed without a scar, and we behold gun-barrels in length and thickness, though of a bore strangely small. No cavity at all would be left by the elongating and compressing wheels were not the bore filled by the foils, which withstand outside pressure. The two sets of rollers each furnish forth a hundred barrels in a day.

No words can paint any adequate picture of the gauntlet a musket-barrel runs. Yet that its career is loner and hard, will be apparent from a list of some few of the operations for which names have been coined. The moment it emerges from the welding-jaws it is plunged for an instant in water, and, while still red-hot, it is straightened on the outside, being laid in a steel couch, which fulfils its mission with a perfection that the proprietors of orthopaedic institutes would be glad if they could equal, or even approach.

Next it is cut off of the right length, as on the bed of Procrustes. It then has a cone-nipple, for holding the percussion cap, inserted into its side. Having been annealed, that it may be softer for tools, it is nut-bored on a boring-bank, that is, a rod, being thrust through it, has a nut fastened on its end, and is gradually pulled back again, so as to enlarge the hole. Having next been smooth-bored by a long gimlet pushed through its whole length, and then straightened on the inside, it is fastened in a lathe and turned like a hoe-handle.

Thence it passes to grinding. This work is done on Nova Scotia stones, the peripheries of which run a mile in a minute. Such stones, each more than a foot thick, weighing over forty quintile, and seven feet in diameter, waste away completely, and perish within two weeks; and the barrels, but for being kept all the while wet, would shoot out broader flames than will ever burst from their muzzles.

Then, sights to help the marksman's aim are brazed upon the barrel. After this long preparatory course, comes proving. The proving-house is a strong cabin in one of the courts. Thirty-two barrels stand in a stack: one man puts a funnel in the muzzles; another pours in powder, from a cup that holds just the proof-charge; a third follows it with a roll of thick paper. Elongated balls are then put in, and pushed home with a six-pound rammed.

The thirty-two are then laid in a separate room, on iron grooves nearly parallel, and pointing into a sandbank; a train of powder is so drawn along as to unite all the touch-holes, the plank doors are shut, and the whole is exploded by a pistol. The proof-charge is about five times as much powder as one for ordinary service. The wad and ball are also heavier. Not one steel barrel in a thousand fails to bear the test; while those of iron are so much inferior, that as many as five in the thirty-two now and then burst. The place of failure is almost always at the line of welding. That sort of work gives way unless done at the very nick of time, when the metal is at exactly the just medium, neither too hot nor yet too cool. Of six hundred and eighty-one iron barrels lately proved, thirteen burst, and ten were condemned for other faults, so that about one in thirty of them were failures.

It sometimes so falls out, that the proof-charge which will not rend a barrel, will so far weaken the metal that it will fly asunder the next time it is fired, even with a smaller charge. To ascertain whether this is the case, the barrels are tried again, with a charge one-fifth lighter than at first. But it is found that very few that stand the first test prove unequal to the second. As has been said, a thousand steel barrels are proof against the larger charge, where one fails. Hence, the prospect of a flaw in a steel barrel, which has endured the first proof, is too slight to rouse much interest in firing it the second time.

Doubtless it is wise to guard against all possibilities that a shooter become an involuntary suicide. Still, the second proof of a steel barrel is not unlike the seeking the living among the dead, as practiced at Frankfort-on-the-Main. In the dead-house there, corpses are laid in a bed, with a thimble on each finger and toe, so arranged that the slightest twitch will ring an alarm-bell. This precaution against premature interment, although long in use, has never yet detected one single individual who needed its aid.

An ordinary day's work for two men, aided a trifle by the United States inspector, will prove about two hundred and fifty-six pieces, for each of which they are each paid one cent.

Nor is this all. Our aspirant to the dignity of an accepted barrel must be "counter-bored" in the breech. As counter-bore is a word you cannot espy either in Webster unabridged and supplemented, or in Worcester, some readers may need to be told that counter-boring is a cut round the head of an orifice, the sides of which are perpendicular to that orifice, instead, as in counter-sinking, of being bevelled down to it. The would-be barrel is next "tapped" with shallow holes, like a sugar-tree. It is then "milled," for squaring or angling the breech. It is "jigged" on its cone-seat.

The operation which follows is of special nicety, and is termed reaming. It is thrice repeated, and performs for the inside of a barrel what polishing afterwards effects for its outside. A wedge of thin paper is here of power to cause a piece to be accepted or rejected. Nor is there anything more beautiful in changeable silk, or the necks of doves, or in the gay creatures of the element that in the colours of the rainbow live, and play in plaited clouds, than in the hues which reaming generates. Our pilgrim tube comes forth from reaming "all glorious within," but it has still not yet attained, neither is perfect.

It is next to be polished. A machine does this service, except that it leaves a few inches at each end to be finished by hand. The value of machines is here brought to view. One machine polishes two hundred barrels a day throughout five-sixths of their length. No less than fourteen men must be busy all the time to complete the single sixth which the machine omits.

Breeching up, deadening or browning, and sometimes rifling, are processes which remain before a barrel can arrive at stocking. In rifling for the United States, only three grooves are cut, and those of uniform width, though growing shallower from breech to muzzle. In those manufactured by the company on its own account, the grooves are seven, of uniform depth, but narrowing from breech to muzzle, as also with a "twist," gaining or graduated. This latter method of rifling is decidedly easier than that required by the Government, and is held by connoisseurs to be in no respect inferior.

The apparatus for rifling is American in origin, of late introduction, was mostly made in the arms factory, and is to a considerable extent in use in no other concern.

On the whole, the barrel machinery sets it careering on such a many-twinkling dance, now advancing, now retreating, as Cowper had in mind when he thus wrote:— "I have read before, of a room with a floor, laid upon springs, and such like things, with so much art in every part, that when you went in, you were forced to begin a minuet pace, with an air and a grace, swimming about, now in and now out, with a deal of state, in a figure of eight, without pipe or string, or any such thing, but making you dance, and as you advance, 'twill keep you still, though against your will, dancing away, alert and gay, with bustling ado, till madam and you are quite worn out in jigging about."

To those who judge by the sight of their eyes, there is no marvel in musket-making comparable to the half reasoning machines which fashion the stocks. These are now sixteen. Receiving a rough and crooked rail, they send it flying through a course of sawing, and centring, and spotting, and first, turning, and barrel-grooving, and profiling, and butt-plating, and letting in the lock, and banding, and working between the bands, and ramrod-grooving, and bedding guard and ramrod spring, and second-turning, and boring and tapping. One is at a loss to decide whether each successive process subtracts more from the weight, or adds more to beauty and adaptations.

These manipulations seem as cruel as the joint-cracking and other terrors of a Turkish bath; and yet, all the *while, they are as safe, salutary, and supp ling, as well as fatal to all clogs on the patient they take in hand.*

These stocking engines are a Yankee notion. They were invented by Thomas Blanchard, who was born at Sutton, Worcester County, Mass., in 1788.

The history and nature of his invention deserve special notice. Mr. Blanchard had devised a lathe to turn musket-barrels with a uniform external finish. Knowledge of this invention came to the superintendent of the Springfield armoury, who contracted for one of the machines. When it was put in operation, one of the workmen remarked that his own work of grinding the barrels was done away with. Another, employed upon the wooden stocks, which were then all made by hand, said that Blanchard could not spoil his job, as he could not make a machine to turn a gunstock. Blanchard answered that he was not sure, but he would think about it; and as he was driving home through the town of Brim field, the idea of his lathe for turning irregular forms suddenly struck him. In his emotion he shouted, "I have got it! I have got it!"

The principle of this machine is, that forms are turned by a pattern having the exact shape of the object to be produced, and which in every part of it is successively brought in contact with a small friction wheel; this wheel precisely regulates the motion of chisels arranged upon a cutting-wheel acting upon the rough block, so that as the friction wheel successively traverses every portion of the rotating pattern, the cutting-wheel pares off the superabundant wood from end to end of the block, leaving a precise facsimile of the model.

The whole sixteen, which, within a generation, have grown from a single germ, were ordered by the British Government for their establishment at Enfield, and the very man, Mr. Caramel Clark, who now manages them here, set them up there, and managed them for more than four years. The only fraction which American machines omitted; some English artisan has added a machine to do. Seventeen engines, then, construct a gunstock, perfect in all essential parts. As they leave it, it is in a shape, as soon as you whittle two or three scarcely perceptible notches for the angles of the barrel and the curve of the breech-pin, a trifle, for doing which no contractor would pay you more than nine mills, all ready to receive lock, barrel, bands, butt-plate, guard, ramrod, and hence to be used in actual warfare.

The stock does not in fact, however, thus receive its mountings. On the other hand, it is spoke-shaved, filed, and sand-papered, with much ado about a very little, for smoothness, fancy, and Government exactions. Here, let it be noted, is a pre-eminent proof how economical machinery approves itself in contrast with hand-labour. The single hand operation, which is a non-essential, both employs twice more men, and costs twice more money, than all the sixteen machine operations, every one of which is essential. The machine is a factotum; the man a do-nothing.

Machine stocks are better than handicrafts men could construct in at least two points; they interchange at will with each other, and they are less liable to be condemned by United States inspectors, as too large or too small. In the Government ideal, the stock is as light as possible consistently with strength, and as strong as possible consistently with lightness.

All deviations from this standard, this bundle of compromises, however trivial, are therefore to be blamed as sins against either lightness or strength. If too heavy, the musket wears out the soldier, as the last peppercorn breaks a camel's back; if too light, its recoil lames his shoulder, like the Hudibrastic gun, which kicked wide and knocked its owner over.

No operation in gun-stocking is more magical than cutting the hole for letting in the lock. A hexagonal frame, No. 1348, is so hung as to turn around above the stock. From each of its corners, as it halts an instant, a tool springs down fiercely, and seems to be tearing the stock in pieces. All the while a blast from two brass pipes blows away the fragments. At the end of forty-five seconds, we behold, hollowed out of the solid wood, a polished cavity of five different depths, and so cunningly fashioned that the most shapeless of all contrivances, a gun-lock, rests and plays in it as in the niche it was ordained to fill.

The black walnut of which stocks are made, used at Springfield to be seasoned for four years. That process is here, by kiln-drying, shortened to but little more than that number of weeks.

On a first ramble through the arms factory, few persons, not of a mechanical turn, scrutinize more than that small fraction of its routine which we have now passed in review. But in every thoughtful mind, curiosity regarding cunning arts is an appetite which grows by what it feeds on. Every member in the arm has a history worth tracing did our limits allow, or could it be made as intelligible in description as it is when surveyed by the eye.

On some visits, we may take a view not so much of anything in particular as of the magnitude of the whole. This is so great that, in 1858, the Secretary of War described it, though not yet half its present size, "as having risen to the dignity of a great national work, as well as superior in machinery and extent to either of the national armoires of the United States."

During the last ten years, it has turned out more weapons than were made or purchased by the British Government in the ten years between 1844 and 1854.

On a general survey of the tout ensemble, we shall linger longest in the armouries proper, that is, in the second stories of the old and of the new edifice. Here are two rooms, each five hundred feet by sixty, each filled with from four to six rows of machines, and around the walls vices enough to hold all the virtues of the handiwork. Toward the river and fields beyond there is a charming outlook, but as one man sometimes tends six machines, there is small opportunity to look out. All work so intensely that they salute no man by the way. From choice they keep that silence which is enforced at Wethersfield and Sins; Sing.

"Within his mouth each doth jail his tongue."

Near evening, however, we fall in with workmen with their sinewy vigour all exhausted, and so ready to talk, lest through overdoing to-day, they become unequal to the task of to-morrow.

We come then into chat with a filer. When a jigging machine has rudely scooped out the shank of a pistol-barrel, it passes into the hands of the first filer, who is paid seven cents for each of those tubes he faithfully rubs something more into shape. His work is hard, and his pay proportionate. From him,

after sundry other manipulations, it comes to the second filer.
He uses seven files, costing in the aggregate $2.29, as bought
of the company at wholesale, and though he cards them clean
a dozen times a day, he wears out two or three sets every month.
He uses them all on the shank, or hook, or sight, and makes on
an average twenty strokes with each. For these one hundred
and forty strokes he is paid but two and a half cents; yet, as one
hundred and fifty barrels daily pass through his hands, his
wages are good. He stamps his initial on each, lest the
inspector send back to him the bad work of another, so that he
would suffer for another's fault.

He has not been long at the business, and would not be
able to do his work, but that he was brought up a machinist.
When he screws up a barrel in a vice, why do not the jaws
scratch it? They are faced with leather stuck on by beeswax.
Through fear of damaging the work, most hammers are made
from a soft alloy of tin and lead, called Rabbit metal.

Few can walk through the armoury without observing
its adroit economies. In the forging department, for instance,
the first thing we see on our right is a ponderous frame called
Dick's shears, which cut off from bars of steel, according to a
gauge, the exact quantum needed for each particular article.
Not a little of raw material is thus saved. Besides, each piece,
having nothing superfluous, comes out of the die so clean as to

be easily trimmed. All the scraps, however small, as well as borings, filings, and shavings, are gathered up and sold. But as this metallic shoddy sells low, yet is as much better than the original article as other shoddy is worse, apparatus is just now preparing for working it over into bars again, in the arms factory itself.

In most cases, the scraps as they fall from the machines are drenched with oil. This union of oil and iron, as Charles Lamb said of mixing brandy and water, spoils two good things. Accordingly, the metallic shavings being collected in a reservoir with a bottom full of holes, they are steamed till the oil is drained off. The steel threads scraped off in rifling resemble wool, and are squeezed in a sort of cheese-press till cleaned of oil. Whenever it is possible, soda-water, being cheaper, is substituted for oil as a cooler and lubricator. There are ten tanks of such water.

But for these and such like devices, the expense of oil would be doubled. How much is thus saved we cannot appreciate, till we count the thirteen cisterns in one row stored with oil, and ascertain that the consumption of it, after all, last year amounted to more than eleven thousand gallons [11,377 1-4 gallons].

Again, for forging an iron barrel, it is necessary to begin with a plate so heavy that a tip, several inches long, is *usually cut off from one end after boring. These tips used to be sold at two cents a pound. But one, or at most two, such tips will make a lock-plate, the iron for which costs eight times as much. Therefore barrel-tips are now kept, and are forged into lock-plates.*

Again, the stocks of many pistols are fabricated of ivory. More than half of each tusk would seem to be wasted while being brought into the fitting shape. Ivory chips, however, and sawdust are not only a better fertilizer than guano; they are a daily necessity in the shop itself, for case-hardening every article which is wrought out of iron.

Yet once more. Cotton waste is indispensable at most machines for wiping them, and the workmen's hands. According to dictionaries, this article is so called "because it is of little or no account or value." Here, it is not only preserved with care, but, when dirty, is washed and used again and again. On the whole, the more we look, the more on every side do we espy economies, those littles which make a mickle, which could never have been thought of but by a Yankee who had full faith in the German superstition, that whatever we leave uneaten on our plate, or unutilized anywhere, is a sacrifice to Satan.

The parts in a rifled musket are eighty-four, and several of them, for describing their genesis, would each require as much space as has been given to the barrel or the stock. At every turn in the workshops we stumble on something new or curious. It is long a mystery how steel can cut steel, and that to all appearance as easily as the softest wood. In such cases the cutter is of harder temper, and its hardness is re-enforced by a diamond shaped point. In making test gauges, where hard steel is to be cut or planed, the tool takes off at once only a very narrow as well as thin shaving. If we watch this process, we shall sometimes find that twenty-seven strokes are required to plane a surface one-eighth of an inch wide.

Other tools, as punches, are greatly larger than what they act on, and so, striking on a steel plate, cut out navy triggers as rapidly as a baker stamps out crackers in dough.

It is no wonder that Col. Colt invented more than one sort of lubricator, to one who marks how much oil is consumed in the construction of arms. Some of the tools could not be tempered aright unless dipped in oil. Of course, there is oil on all wheels, whether on engines below, or on machines above. How it would clog all arms-making here, did we hold with Brazilians, that that it is impossible to drive away devils without leaving all wheels greased and creaking! There is oil on all bright iron, lest it rust; oil on all tools, and the metals they cut, to guard against heat, and the friction, technically called "grinding," of borings, shavings, and parings. On the *inside of a gunstock there is sperm oil to soften it; on its outside there is linseed oil to harden it. In manifold delicate manoeuvres, it is clear that the oil, so trifling in quantity, and so mild in its action as not to be noticed, makes the difference not merely between facility and difficulty, but between facility and failure.*

On many machines we see brushes, sell-moved, which remove all rubbish, so that it cannot obstruct the tools. Most machines are automatic, or self-guided, stop when they have finished their task, and some of them are said to do so whenever anything is deranged, so that if they go ahead, they must go wrong. They must be sure they are 'right, or they will not go ahead.

Including screws, there are twenty-eight pieces in a pistol, and three times as many in a regulation musket. Most of them, viewed singly, seem useless. Indeed, they are so. Their value is apparent only when they are fitly joined together in one organic whole compacted of many parts, all mutually related, E pluribus unum. Their strength, like that of the old man's fagot in Aesop, lies in the band that unites them. It will move our special wonder in the assembling-room, where dead fractions are vivified, to see how readily, after a slight touch with a file, and more often without any fitting, pieces taken at random from heaps of the same sort, fit into each other. It reminds of the reunions at the resurrection, or of Solomon's temple, "the house which, when it was in building, was built of stone made ready before it was brought thither, so that there was neither hammer, nor axe, nor any tool of iron, heard in the house while it was in building."

How is such an "assembling" possible? Because all the bits of the same name have been formed in the same die, or cast in the same mould, and measured with the same exactitude, by the self-same gauges.

As long ago as the Mexican war, so exquisite was the adaptation of member to member, that three fourths of the broken arms picked up on a field of battle, interchanged so as to furnish forth serviceable weapons again. This matter of interchange deserves the more notice, because it has been both exaggerated and underrated.

It is not easy to exaggerate the readiness of interchange in the parts of a musket. So we shall judge when we have stood by the assembler, seen him pick up the pieces at hap-hazard, clap them together, and fasten them by eleven screws, and all within three minutes. That the members composing a pistol may each find in another its counterpart, some slight manipulations may be needed. Yet the system of correspondences has never been carried further than here, no, not in Swedenborg's Heavenly Arcana.

It is no rhetorical flourish to say, that parts into parts reciprocally shoot as perfectly as Leibniz could imagine them in his doctrine of Pre-established Harmony. Accordingly, orders come every day for some single piece, barrel, hammer, trigger, or lock-frame, to replace one that has failed. Such orders are given, and filled out, with well-grounded confidence that the new-comer will at once find itself at home in its new position, though a thousand leagues away, and in an arm fabricated years ago. There is then a practical advantage resulting from rendering each element in a weapon a fac-simile of the analogous element in every other of its class. Again, if a model piece is the beau ideal in size and form, all deviations from either, however infinitesimal, are so far faulty and reprehensible.

The metallic portions are of course of the same weight, so that when an artisan has finished a day's work of several .thousand bolts, for instance, and is paid so much a hundred for them, he has only to count a single hundred, and then ascertain by scales how many times as much as that hundred his whole quantity weighs.

It will still be asked, "If such permutations and combinations be possible, why is a number stamped upon each pistol six times over?" Partly because pieces which have been once matched in the assembling-room, unite with rather less *ado than others; partly also to show how many have been made, and facilitate the keeping of accounts; and in great part to aid in identifying stolen goods. This expedient to stop a thief is analogous to what is termed "rogue's yarn," that is, yarn of a different twist and colour, which is inserted in all the cordage of the British navy, to identify it if stolen. The boys who bring workmen their dinner, now and then snap up a screw, or bolt, or trigger, as an unconsidered trifle; then go on to pilfer a stock, or cylinder, or barrel. When they have secured all the eight and twenty component parts, they assemble them in a pistol. But such a picnic arm, wherever seen, betrays itself by lacking the number, which is not stamped in the factory until all the parts are united. More than one theft having been thus detected, such thieving has hence become rare.*

These pistol-stealers would have eluded the detectives, could they have erased the numbers from half the revolvers in Hartford, repeating the ruse of a certain French page. This scapegrace, when caught in the chamber of a maid of honour, had managed to escape unrecognized, but with the loss of his badge. Next morning, all the pages were called before the major-domo, to see which of them had no badge. None of them had any, for the guilty one had gone to the dormitory of his companions, and, while they were asleep, had abstracted all their badges. Seldom has necessity been mother of so artful a dodge. Again, when it was once inquired in court whether certain cases of arms had been stolen from the United States, it was proved that they must have been, by the numbers on them corresponding to those recorded on the books of the company as sold to the Government.

Before being "assembled," or combined in one, each individual portion of each arm is inspected. In Japan, all cross-eyed men inherit as their birth right the office of spies, for all who have that peculiarity of vision are viewed as "fellows by the hand of nature marked, quoted, and signed" to do a Paul Pry's work. In like manner, inspectors ought to be selected from the most thorough paced grumblers, or what Hood calls "hedgehogs rolled up the wrong way," so that their duties and inclinations may all point in the same direction. Their duty is to cavil on the ninth part of a hair.

We take up a tumbler which has already stood the ordeal six times, and drop it into a gauge. It slides in like the noiseless flow of oil from a flask, and sets so tight that it will not rattle. Yet it is rejected. Why so? Simply because on one side it fails to fill the gauge-socket so far that you can thrust in a corner of a bit of silk paper. When the inspector tries a barrel, his gauge must sink in without friction, yet touch it at every point, so that the air compressed below will hold up the bar of steel, and, if you force it down, will toss it up again.

He has a block of lead on which he hammers triggers set up edgewise, to see if they will break. Lock-frames he knocks against this block, and, if they ring dull and lumpish, condemns them as lacking a tight base-pin. Cone-nipples he twirls on an awl, and throws them out if it goes through beyond a certain point, or does not reach it. If any chamber in a cylinder falls short a hair's breadth of the standard depth, he sends it to be bored again.

Occasionally, a scar in the lock-frame which mars not its efficiency, is winked at by the company's officials, but it finds no mercy among those sent hither from Washington. Now and then, those dressed in a little brief authority play such fantastic tricks that they are compared to that stupid ship-captain who boxed the compass for a week round a shoal which was at length found to be an imaginary danger, namely, a fly-blow on his chart. Here the inspector has condemned a revolver which to our eyes is perfect. Why is it not? Because one shaving too much was pared off on one side of the back-strap. The inspector has also cut an ugly notch in its stock, and if we ask him why, answers, "That I may know it again. If I did not nick it, they would send it back to me once more, and when the defect is very slight and microscopical, I might accept to-morrow what I have rejected to-day, and should then be laughed at for inconsistency. How often, with accidental variations, men repeat the experience of those riotous youth, who, when King Philip gave judgment against them, appealed, and when he asked "To whom?" said, "From Philip drunk to Philip sober."

But, trifling apart, the United States inspectors ought to be hypercritical, lest by any possibility an arm pass muster with them, and yet fail when it cannot be repaired, or in the heat of battle, when its failure is likely to cost a life. Hence, few officials deserve their salaries better than the six-and-twenty professional fault-finders whom the Government here maintains. With reason also are this corps transferred, at short and uncertain intervals, from armoury to armoury, that they may not be open to bribes, or worth bribing.

Nor need Colt's arms shrink from any test, however rigid, for they have obtained from the Secretary of War's censors as good a report as those of any other manufacture, whether private or national. Indeed, four muskets here made have been accepted by the Government as models, and sent as standards to contractors at other armouries in four different States.

Yet have not our authorities, after all, been penny wise but pound foolish? While so scrupulous about muskets, they have been negligent about the men who shall handle our armies.

Cadets have been admitted at West Point, because franked thither by members of Congress, or because the pets of higher functionaries, not because they have given tokens of capacity to excel in military science. Had that school been open to those only who, in the fair field of competitive examinations, could prove themselves worthiest, how much more ably would our forces now be officered! How much more grateful, hopeful, and serviceable would be the task of its instructional corps! Had its doors opened only to receptive minds, its professors would never have been expected to carve marble statues out of snow, or, according to the proverb, to make a silk purse out of a sow's ear.

Such is a meagre sketch of some characteristics of what may be styled the cornucopia of Mars, the establishment in which fire-arms of the best model were first fabricated on a grand scale in the United States by a private company. Col. Colt lies buried near his house, in a thicket of evergreens, and beneath a plain marble slab. But his simple tomb is in full view of the arms factory, which is his true monument. Before his death, and through his energetic genius, it had become substantially what it is to-day.

The volleys in the proving-house daily sound his requiem. Si monument um requires, circumspect!

The Charter Oak

Although Colt was always critical of the taxes he was expected to pay, a theme that continued throughout his life, he was always among the first to demand various improvements to public facilities.

His pet project was the establishment of a public park on Wyllys Hill. This was where the Charter Oak stood, a tree that legend had it was where captain Joseph Wadsworth hid the charter of the Connecticut Colony when Governor Edmund Andros tried to seize it. The tree became a symbol of American independence.

Colt offered to purchase the necessary land for the park, provided the City or the State would guarantee its upkeep but it was pointed out to Colt that the cost of purchasing the land was nothing compared to the ongoing cost of its upkeep, so Samuel's offer was declined.

The Charter Oak

Painting by Charles De Wolfe Brownel 1857

The Charter Oak was part of Samuel's life, he had played in it as a child and been fascinated by the legend ever since he learned of it at his mother's knee, so when it blew down on August 21st 1856 he was devastated. It was largely due to Samuel's suggestion that the owner of Wyllys Hill, one I. W. Stuart, presented enough of the wood from it to the city so that they could have a chair made for the use of the mayor.

The council commissioned John H. Most, a master carver and cabinet maker to construct the chair and what he produced was truly a work of art.

The city fathers were delighted with the result of Most's work, but not with his bill of $375. They tried to haggle but Most insisted they either pay or give up any claim to the chair, and since the wood had cost them nothing, they gave up their claim to it in good faith.

Reading between the lines at this time in Samuel Colt's life, it seems that a resentment of the way he had been viewed and treated in the past had emerged. The early struggles to go his own way, the difficulties he had in gaining interest in his invention, the disputes with cousin Dudley, the treachery of Ehlers and Whitney and the constant lack of money coming from those in power with no foresight had taken their toll.

It also seems that although Samuel had managed to integrate back into social circles on his return to Hartford, he didn't feel that he had received the recognition from the city elders that he deserved. He felt that they should have killed the fatted calf much more than they did when the prodigal son made good had returned.

Samuel took the opportunity to get his own back on the council by not only paying for the Charter Oak Chair himself, but by rebuking the council for their apparent lack of respect for the area's history.

To most of the residents of Hartford the Charter Oak had simply been an old tree. It was rotting anyway, so the wind had in fact saved them the trouble of cutting it down, but Samuel made sure that the history of the old tree was widely publicised.

Charter Oak Chair

He not only planted seedlings on his property that had been grown from the acorns of the old tree, holding elaborate ceremonies for each planting, he also named a recreation centre that he built on his land for his workers, "Charter Oak Hall." This was all part of an elaborate plan to make Wyllys Hill a public park with a suitable memorial to the ancient oak.

In the end Samuel's campaign raised considerable feeling against the council for not purchasing the Charter Oak Chair, but it also created new enemies for Colt himself.

Wood from the tree was in demand from other quarters as well and the state of Connecticut had a high backed "Chair of State" made. It was paid for and is still used today by the Lieutenant Governor in the state senate chamber.

Samuel Colt was a remarkable man who achieved a great many things in his life, but sadly, the establishment of a public park on Wyllys Hill was never one of them, and it was one of his biggest regrets.

Chair of State

Made from wood of the Charter Oak

Employee Welfare

Samuel Colt's concepts about the way things should be done were not limited to his ideas of mass production and assembly lines, of which he was a pioneer. He also had radical ideas about the way workers should be treated.

He believed that his employees should live near their place of work and to this end he built on his estate a group of four-family houses that were the last word in comfort and convenience. He believed that workmen enjoyed their leisure time more if they could go home free of factory dirt and grime, so he provided basins, soap, towels and hot water throughout his armoury for the use of his workers.

In the matter of working hours, he had his own ideas as well. Between twelve and thirteen hours was the normal working day at the time, but Samuel didn't think a man could give of his best for that period of time, especially if doing mundane menial or repetitive tasks, so he stipulated that none of his workers would be permitted to work more than ten hours a day and that each man should take one hour for his lunch.

Some of the younger workers, no doubt with an eye to having more leisure time in the evenings, suggested a thirty-minute noon break and an earlier finish but Colt wouldn't permit it.

"Only fools or slaves would gulp their midday meal in half an hour," he declared, *"and I want neither in my employ."*

Many of the parts that made up Samuel's revolver were produced on a contract system, where the contractor was required to produce a specified number of items at a pre-agreed price. Workmen were then employed on a piecework basis by the contractors.

The system was open to abuse. Some contractors would encourage workers to work faster with the lure of large earnings and then, after sacking a few of the slower ones to create fear of losing their jobs in the others, they would reduce the price paid and increase their own profit.

Colt made it clear to his contractors that he would not tolerate such practices. He set a minimum price and no contractor was permitted to pay less. Men could be sacked only with the approval of Samuel's general manager, and if Samuel was in Hartford, they also had the right of appeal to him personally.

Colt also built for his workforce a social centre, the Charter Oak Hall, which was a meeting hall that could also be used as a ballroom or theatre. It had recreation and reading rooms that were supplied with games, books, newspapers and periodicals and was where Samuel encouraged discussions to take place. From time to time he also arranged art exhibitions, lectures, fairs, plays and he even organised a band from among his employees, supplying all the instruments and uniforms himself.

If Samuel had visions of a Samuel Colt band playing at ceremonies and functions, however, he was to be disappointed. Despite the fact that he had hired a tutor, his workforce struggled to master the extremely expensive brass instruments that he had purchased for them. Even Samuel, on hearing the attempts to play, realised that there was little hope of improvement.

Another Venture

In building his dyke to keep the Connecticut river off his land, Samuel had imported willow from Holland and the crop had flourished. One day, a stranger called at Armsmear and offered to purchase the entire crop.

It turned out that the stranger was in fact a manufacturer of willow furniture and he was of the opinion that Samuel's crop of willow was better quality than the willow he had been importing from Holland.

Samuel put the man off, simply stating that the crop was not for sale, but his visit had planted the germ of an idea in Samuel's mind. He began making enquiries about the willow furniture business and it didn't take him long to realise that it was very inefficient in its operation. Its overheads were way too high and he was convinced that anyone moving into the business who could improve efficiency would be able make a good profit, especially if he grew his own willow.

Samuel looked into recruiting skilled willow workers but found that he would have to entice them away from their present employers. Realising that such a move would cause resentment and problems in the labour market he decided against it.

Instead, he wrote to his German agent, C. F. Wappenhans and ordered that workers be recruited there. Wappenhans advised Samuel that the willow workers in Germany and Holland lived in communes and that none of them would be prepared to leave their particular hamlet without their relatives and friends.

It might be possible to move an entire community, including livestock, to Hartford, but Wappenhans went on to explain that the workers were set in their ways and would not be happy in a strange environment with new customs and strange houses.

Samuel requested complete details of the workers' houses, along with their customs and habits, he demanded accurate drawings of their houses and of the community at play.

Wappenhans sent Samuel all the information he could about the houses, customs and habits of a small community of workers near Potsdam. These people worked on a communal bases, with each taking great pride in their work.

They were not interested in earning great sums of money, all they wanted was to earn enough to eat and clothe themselves, they had no need of luxuries. To them, life was for living not working, and living was eating and drinking, music and song.

Of the many drawings and descriptions of the workers at play that Wappenhans sent Samuel, by far the most interesting ones to Samuel, showed them singing and playing music in a band or orchestra.

Samuel was delighted, the tutor that he had hired to teach his workers to play the instruments he had purchased was becoming more and more frustrated with the lack of progress, as was Samuel himself. Here was a group of workers who seemed to have music in their very souls. Soon perhaps, with people like these in his employ, his workforce could put on a performance that would impress the good folk of Hartford.

He ordered Wappenhans to gather up the Hamlet of Potsdam and send the men, women and children to Hartford and to reassure them that by the time they arrived a reproduction of their Hamlet in Potsdam would be waiting for them, including a beer garden and a bandstand.

It took some months of coaxing to persuade the inhabitants of Potsdam to move all the way to Hartford, but move they did, lock, stock and barrel.

Almost as soon as they arrived, Colt organised a concert to entertain the good people of Hartford, and he was overjoyed by the quality of the music his new workers provided. It wasn't long before Colt's band was as famous in New England as his revolver.

Colt's Potsdam houses and willow works 1860

Colt was more than pleased with his new workers as musicians, but their working practices were a nightmare to him. It was their practice, as it had been for generations, for each man to make a piece of furniture complete from start to finish, including the splitting and peeling of the willow to start and the application of the final coat of shellac to finish. To rub salt into Samuel's wounds, every operation was performed by hand!

After studying the work for a while, Samuel realised that many of the tasks could be done, as well if not better, by machine.

First, he invented a device that would split and peel the willow much quicker and cleaner than could be done by hand.

The workers could see Samuel's thinking behind the device and because it performed the task well, they accepted it, but when he started turning up with seat and back frames that were already cut and shaped ready to be assembled, they feared that they were going to be replaced by his machines and objected strongly.

Samuel overcame their objection, by agreeing to pay them the same piecework price per item of furniture built from the machine prepared frames, as they were getting for the hand-made pieces. As this enabled them to earn more for the same hours of work, it didn't take them long to get used to that as well.

Gradually Colt managed to get his workers to accept more of his working practises, meaning that he was able to increase output, lower costs and importantly, increase wages. Within a few years of his workers arriving, they were earning more money than others in the industry and Colt was selling his furniture at lower prices. His furniture was for sale as far west as California and as far south as Cuba.

Chapter Thirteen

Marriage and Children

When the building of Armsmear was in full swing, Samuel's long courtship of Miss Elizabeth Jarvis ended in marriage during a hot hazy New England afternoon on the 5th June 1856.

Elizabeth Jarvis was a beautiful woman, who came from a wealthy family with strong views based on piety, respect and obligation. Born on 5th October 1826, she was twelve years younger than Samuel. Elizabeth had lived with an aunt in Hartford in the 1840s and had attended school in the town.

The wedding ceremony was held inside the parlour of the Jarvis family's Middletown residence, by the same Episcopal bishop who had married Elizabeth's parents decades earlier.

It was a spectacular affair that day as Samuel had determined it would be. The entire wedding party boarded the steamboat "Washington Irving" at Samuel's armoury and as it left the jetty, draped in flags and bunting, a grand salute of rifles was fired from the armoury's cupola. Samuel was determined that no one who witnessed his wedding would ever forget it.

It was estimated that Elizabeth's dress and jewellery cost upwards of $8,000, an extraordinary amount of money in those days and all of it supplied by Samuel Colt. As a wedding present Samuel gave his bride a necklace and matching earrings created by his friend, Charles Tiffany of Tiffany & Company. The 38.84-carat-weight necklace consisted of blue enamel links set with 20 mine-cut diamonds interspersed with smaller diamonds.

Necklace and earrings Samuel gave to Elizabeth as a wedding gift.
The actual necklace is in the Museum of Fine Arts, Boston

The cake stood six feet high and was covered in fondant pistols and rifles and surmounted by a figure of Colt himself. The reception was held in New York at the St. Nicholas, one of the most impressive and expensive hotels in the city.

The next day Samuel and Elizabeth, together with Elizabeth's sister Hetty and her brother Richard, set sail for Europe. They spent a month in London before moving on to Belgium, Bavaria, Vienna, Holland and Russia, a grand tour where they were greeted as ambassadors at every stop.

Money was no object of course, Colt's company was doing exceptional business and Samuel knew, as did most of his countrymen by then, that America was heading for a civil war, and although Samuel was no war monger and hated the thought of his countrymen fighting each other, he didn't expect arms sales to diminish in such a situation.

Samuel Colt must have felt on top of the world, after all, he had fulfilled his childhood dream of making his fortune by becoming an inventor. He was now a multi-millionaire with a beautiful wife and a beautiful home, all he needed now was an heir.

The couple were delighted when they learned that Elizabeth was pregnant, but the baby, Samuel Jarvis Colt, was born prematurely on 24th February 1857.

I. W. Stuart, the owner of Wyllys Hill and the man who had given the wood from the Charter Oak to make the mayor's chair, now presented Samuel and Elizabeth with a cradle for their new arrival, made from the wood of that same tree.

Along with the cradle was a letter addressed to and intended for the infant, detailing the history of the Charter oak.

"Hartford, April 25, 1857.

Master Samuel Jarvis Colt:- You are a tiny infant now, Sammy, just bursting into life, and cannot read or understand what I write you at the present time. But you will grow, and will be able to read and understand it by and by, and then you will find out that a friend of your father and mother and to you, sent for you this day a beautiful present, a cradle for you to rock in when you were a baby, and a cradle made from the wood of a very famous tree called the Charter Oak.

This tree is famous, Sammy, because a long time ago, when the state in which you were born was as young almost as you are now, a very bad man, named Edmond Androids, came with a troop of soldiers to the town in which you first saw the light, and tried to take away from the good people there, a long parchment roll which was called the Charter of Connecticut.

Now, this Charter made the people of whom I speak a very free people. It gave them Liberty, and liberty, you will live, I hope, to learn, Sammy, is a very precious thing, and ought to be defended at the cost of all the money in the world...yes, and at the cost, too, sometimes of human life.

But the people of whom I speak were few in number and weak, and no match at all in power for the man who came to take away their Charter, for this bad man was backed by a great tyrant king, who lived far away across the rolling sea, and who had armies and navies big enough to crush the little settlement in which these people lived, forever. So Edmond Audios thought he was sure of getting the Charter, because these people were weak, and he and his master were strong, and he went, therefor, with a file of soldiers into a large room, called the Court Chamber, where the government and Deputy Governor, and the great men of these people were assembled...there he went to take the Charter.

But just as he moved forward to a large round table on which the Charter lay, and was stretching out his hand to snatch it, the candles in the chamber were all suddenly blown out, as quick as thought, and a very brave, patriotic man, named captain Joseph Wadsworth, who loved the people and the liberty of which I speak, seized the Charter himself, in the midst of the darkness, and running with it as swift as a deer, just as you will run, I hope, by and by, Sammy, he hid it in the hollow of a beautiful great oak; and when the candles in the chamber where Edmond Androids was , were lighted up again, lo Sammy, the Charter em gone! And Androids couldn't find it anywhere, and never did, and the people of whom I speak were happy again, and rejoiced because their liberty was saved by means of this beautiful great oak, and they loved this oak forever after.

Now Sammy, your cradle is made out of the wood of this beautiful great oak, and it should teach you always to remember that hero who hid the Charter so well, and make you follow his example in defending your country whenever it is in danger. Die for your native land, rather than let anybody hurt it!

The cradle too should teach you to be wise and virtuous and honourable and industrious just as those good men were who lived when the Oak was made so famous. They thought it was best always to do right...so always think yourself.

They adored liberty...so do you always adore liberty. They worshipped justice...so do you always worship justice. They made truth their idol...so do you always make truth your idol. They worked out their own prosperity...in other words, these good men of the olden time, "paddled their own canoes"...so always do yourself, and mark it, Sammy. That I caused your cradle to be made in the shape of a beautiful canoe, in order to remind you of this sterling duty.

Your father thought a great deal of this duty, and he acted it out, and once told a committee of the lofty British Parliament that he "paddled his own canoe" Sammy, remember it!

But first and last and best of all, my little friend, those good men of whom I speak, who lived in the days when the oak of which your cradle is made first became famous, loved God, that great and good being above us, far up in the golden skies, who take care of us all and wants us all to love him, and if we do, will make us all happy. Sammy, love God, love your father and mother, love your Aunt Hettie, who is all the time now finding pretty dimples in your cheeks, love all your kindred, love all mankind. Be virtuous Sammy, as your father often says, and then you will certainly be happy, and go some day and see God.

From the old proprietor of the Oak and your true friend.
I. W. Stuart.

When Stuart wrote in his letter that one day Samuel Jarvis would go to see God, he could have had no idea that the event was to happen only eight months after presenting the proud parents with the cot.

Elizabeth, who often referred to God as, The Good Shepherd, wrote soon after, *"For ten months the bright, loving little baby made new sunshine in our happy home; but when he had made himself so tenderly beloved, he was, after a short but painful illness borne so patiently, gathered into the arms of the Good Shepherd."*

Elizabeth often talked about the wonder and grandeur of their home at Armsmear that Samuel's fame and fortune had bestowed on them, but described it as becoming *"a very desolate place to be without the child's bubbly spirit around to liven it up."*

Cradle intended for Samuel Jarvis Colt made from wood of the Charter Oak.
Courtesy of Wadsworth Atheneum Museum of Art

While Elizabeth worked hard looking after their home, Samuel busied himself with business, defending his patents and taking out new ones on new models of pistols and after a while the couple tried for another child.

They were soon blessed with the birth of Caldwell Hart Colt, named after his two great grandfathers, on 24th November 1858. Delighted to have a child in the house again they decided that one was not enough and Elizabeth Jarvis Colt arrived on the scene in 1860.

In the summer of that same year, the family travelled to Nantucket and Martha's Vineyard for a holiday, chartering a boat to take them from the armoury downriver into the Atlantic Ocean and on to Cape Cod.

The couple were happy once more, young Caldwell was strong and healthy and little Elizabeth, or Lizzie as she was known, was the darling of her father's eye. Business was booming and all was well in Colt's world. But the fates are often cruel, and possibly deciding that a gunmaker was not entitled to such happiness, they were to deal Samuel Colt and his family another crushing blow, for no sooner had they returned home, than little Lizzie fell ill.

In Elizabeth Colt's words, *"When the chill October winds were blowing,* Lizzie *folded her pale hands and closed the dear eyes forever."*

One cannot imagine how hard the death of little Lizzie must have hit them both, coming so soon after the death of their first child. As a religious man, Samuel must have wondered if he was maybe being punished by God for arming the world with his guns.

It is reported, that after the mourners had filed past the body of little Lizzie, laying in her little coffin covered in flowers, Samuel took a portrait of her and sat with it for hours in total abject grief, unable to speak.

The burial service was performed by the same minister who had poured water on her head in baptism and Elizabeth wrote, talking of her husband, *"He, who had borne unflinchingly every ill and burden of life, sank down before the open grave of the guileless babe, and for weeks did not leave his room."*

Samuel's body was laid so low by the death of his beloved Lizzie that he succumbed to a debilitating bout of gout. He knew that for him, the only one way to deal with physical or emotional pain was to work, and so for the next three months he managed his empire from Armsmear.

In February 1861, hoping that a change of surroundings and a better climate would ease his gout, Samuel and Elizabeth sailed with young Caldwell to Cuba.

Caldwell was only two years old but even so he seemed to enjoy the voyage and as a young man, in later years, he developed a love of sailing.

End game

When the couple returned from Cuba, Civil War had broken out as expected. Samuel's condition required rest, but rest was not in his nature, orders for his guns were flooding in and he worked tirelessly overseeing the expansion of his factory to cope with demand.

Samuel took no delight in the expansion of his factory at that time, that fact that the country was divided and fighting troubled him greatly. He had always been a democrat and a firm supporter of his personal friend Stephen Douglas.

At forty-six years of age he was not an old man, but the deaths of so many who were close to him, his sisters, his dear brother John and two of his three children had taken their toll, and now thousands of his countrymen were killing each other with his invention. It was a heavy burden to bear, and his health suffered.

The birth of his second daughter, however, Henrietta Seldon, on May 23rd 1816, brought some joy back into his life. Samuel had never stopped working, not through the sadness of loss nor though the pain of illness and his company continued to expand.

Orders for pistols in 1856 had been 24,053 and that had increased to nearly 39,000 the following year and in 1861 an incredible 69,655 pistols had been sold along with 3,193 for a rifle Samuel had been perfecting. The Civil War would take the total in 1862 to 111,676.

Surely now, Samuel and Elizabeth Colt could look forward to a future where their family could flourish and be free of grief, but the fates were not finished them yet and even more tragedy was lurking in the wings.

That winter, Samuel went down with a very bad cold and suffered a return of the gout that had laid him so low before, and he spent much of the Christmas holiday in bed.

Elizabeth nursed him daily, seeing to his every need as well as running the household, which was no small task.

When the new year came, it found Samuel well enough to sit up in bed and receive a few visitors. On 4th January, Elizabeth went out, it's unknown where.

She was very much the Mistress of Armsmear by now and was known as the matriarch of Connecticut's capital city.

When she returned, the staff immediately informed her that her husband had asked for the bible his father had given him as a child. It seems that Samuel was in the habit of placing things in his bible that inspired him, and on this occasion, it was a piece of poetry that he had cut out of a newspaper. Elizabeth commented later that it must have *"touched an answering chord in his soul, as he had no particular fondness for poetry."*

From then, Samuel's health deteriorated still further and there were times when he seemed to lose his reason. Elizabeth herself saw to his nursing needs and sat beside the bed reading to him.

The next morning Elizabeth tells us, he woke in a more cheerful mood and at one o'clock, servants helped Samuel to get up and dress as he wanted to spend some time with the children.

When playing with his children, Samuel appeared briefly to suffer a loss of his senses and from that time on he was not in his right frame of mind, although Elizabeth was convinced that Samuel was just as aware of the changes in his condition as she was. Both hoped and prayed that it was a temporary condition but nevertheless they sent a telegraph to Samuel''s friend, Dr. John F. Gray, in New York, summoning him to Armsmear.

Dr. Gray arrived at noon on 7th January 1862. That evening, Samuel talked uninterrupted for two or three hours but his words were unintelligible and it was clear that whatever ailed him was affecting his mind.

Many speak of the swan-song, a period of peace that comes over the dying just before their final moments and this appears to have come to Samuel. *"The clouds were lifted,"* Elizabeth wrote, *"and he looked off into the great unknown future with a calm serenity and beautifully and touchingly spoke."*

"Death is very near. I trust in God's love and mercy. I have strived to do right according to my sense of right, though all things look differently to me now with my end so near. I forgive all who have injured me."

Samuel had always believed that people had conspired against him but he wanted Elizabeth to know that he was not leaving the world holding any grudges, he had succeeded in spite of all that had been put in his way and he would die in peace.

Samuel spoke to Elizabeth of their children as she recalls, *"confiding our boy to my tenderest care and love; bidding me keep that tender little one, so soon to be fatherless, from all evil, to teach him all the good, with the solemn earnestness only those can command who stand between the seen and the unseen, the living and the dead."*

And now we have to trust that Elizabeth's memory of the occasion is fully accurate and honest, because she goes on to say that Samuel was able at this time to make an astonishing prediction.

"Our bright, sweet baby is going too, and doesn't need to be kept from evil,"

"It was as if Samuel was speaking to the Shepherd of the lambs," said Elizabeth, *"and relating those prophetic thoughts back to me."* The child Henrietta, Samuel went on to say, *"soon would gather her untried soul into His own fold, to be blessed forever."*

Samuel bid Elizabeth to carry out his plans as far as she was able and said his farewell to the wife he loved dearly, saying, *"When God wills, you should go to me beyond the grave, where partings never enter."*

He did not die that day however but lingered on through two more days of pain, until on the morning of Friday 10th January 1862, Samuel Colt finally went to meet his wife's Good Shepherd.

If Samuel mentioned his possible illegitimate son in Germany during his last days, Elizabeth never spoke of it. Samuel had been sending money to Caroline, who had by then changed her name to Julia Leicester, for the care and education of young Samuel, who would have been twenty at the time of Colt's death and was now considering a move to the United States.

The funeral of Samuel Colt took place on the 14th January 1862 and was described by Ellsworth Grant, *"The funeral of Samuel Colt, America's first great munitions maker, was spectacular, certainly the most spectacular ever seen in Hartford, Connecticut...like the last act of a grand opera."*

Both the coffin and the gravestone bore the inscription, *"Kindest husband, father, and friend, adieu."*

Besides the hundreds of employees, thousands of mourners passed through Armsmear for three straight days honouring the great man, and Samuel was buried in the grounds of Armsmear next to his children, Samuel Jarvis and Little Lizzie. Caldwell Colt stood by his mother's side.

In his will Samuel set aside a large area of land on which a school was to be built to teach mechanics and engineering.

Extract from Samuel Colt's will

"I give, devise, and bequeath to the following persons, viz.: to the Governor of the State of Connecticut for the time

being, to the Secretary of the said State for the time being, to the Commissioner of the School Fund for the time being, the Mayor of the city of Hartford for the time being; the President of the Connecticut Historical Society for the time being, the Superintendent of the Colt Patent Fire-Arms Manufacturing Company for the time being, the Engineer of the State for the time being, the engineer of the city of Hartford for the time being, and Isaac W. Stuart, Henry Barnard, Henry C. Deming, and Richard D. Hubbard, of the said city of Hartford, and to their successors as hereinafter provided, twenty-five hundred shares of the stock of said Colt's Patent Fire-Arms Manufacturing Company; also a certain square of land in the southwestern corner of the Hartford, within the dykes recently constructed in the South Meadow, and bounded easterly on Van Dyke Avenue, southerly on Wawarme Avenue, westerly on Hendrickson Avenue, and northerly on Wasseek Street; also a lot of the land on the South side of said Wawarme Avenue and without the dyke, opposite said square of land above described, and to be of the same size and shape, and within corresponding lines, together with all the tract of land which lies between said two squares of land above described and Connecticut River; the premises hereby devised are laid down on said map of land hereunto annexed, to have and to hold them, the several persons above described, and their successors, as trustees, for the following purposes,, uses, and trusts, viz: for the foundation and establishment of a school or institution for the instruction and education of young men in practical mechanics and engineering."

He went on to say how the money was to be split between building the school and supplying it with books and equipment and continued,

"The institution hereby founded shall be open to such young men as said trustees shall see fit to admit; but my desire is that preference should be given by said trustees to the sons of the men who are or have been in my employ, or in the employ of said Colt's Patent Firearms Manufacturing Company, next to inhabitants of the state of Connecticut, and lastly to such other pupils as the trustees shall see fit to admit, on payment of adequate rates for tuition and instruction and so forth.

All pupils belonging to this State who shall be admitted by said trustees, shall, if able to pay the expenses of their education in the said institution, give such obligation, bond or security as said trustees shall see fit to require, for the repayment to the said trustees of said education, whenever, after leaving said institution, they shall be able to do so.

All pupils from this State who are of sufficient ability, and all pupils from other States, shall pay such rates for tuition as said trustees shall prescribe. The pupils in said institution

shall be dressed in appropriate uniform, and their time, with due and reasonable allowance for healthy sports and recreation, shall be equally divided between theoretical studies and mechanics and engineering and practical employment in the workshop."

The world would remember Samuel Colt for his inventions and for the great arms manufacturing empire he had built, but it seems clear that Samuel himself wanted to leave behind some great institution that would remind people of his good works as well.

Tragedy it would seem was never far away from Samuel Colt and his loved ones and just ten days after a grief-stricken Elizabeth had laid her husband in his grave, Samuel's death bed prediction came true and little Henrietta was laid to rest next to her sister and father.

Elizabeth had been pregnant when Samuel had died and it was not long after the funeral that she miscarried.

Elizabeth must have felt that she and Samuel between them had suffered more grief and misfortune than anyone deserved or could bear. Little did she know, but more was to follow.

Two years after Samuel's death, in 1864, the Colt Armoury burnt to the ground destroying over $800.00 worth of machinery and probably half that value in stock, together with many original models of Samuel's pistols.

No one knows what actually caused the fire, but with the civil war still raging there was plenty of talk of Confederate arson, but the fact that cotton waste was often to be found near drive-pulleys and that the floorboards would have been soaked in oil, a spark is just as good, if not a better, explanation of the cause.

Samuel Colt had not been a believer in insurance and had never had the building covered, Elizabeth on the other hand had different views on the subject and took out a policy shortly after Samuel's death, however, it was not enough to cover the full cost of rebuilding, but it was rebuilt, and this time with decent fire precautions in place.

Elizabeth couldn't run the Colt Armoury on her own so she relied heavily on Elisha Root who was not just an employee but a good friend. Elisha died in 1865 however and Elizabeth turned to William Buel Franklin.

With the Armoury being well managed, Elizabeth, who was still grieving for her husband and children, turned her attention to building a church in the grounds of Armsmear. There were now only two things that really mattered to

Elizabeth, building her "Church of the Good Shepherd" and watching young Caldwell grow into a god-fearing young man.

The church was built mainly for the workforce of the armoury and their families but I'm sure that none were turned away.

The Church of the Good Shepherd

Collie, as Caldwell Colt became known, celebrated his twenty-first birthday on 24th November 1879. He showed no interest in, nor talent for, the business of his late father, but rather preferred sailing and had become a yachtsman of some renown, and a highly competitive sportsman.

He soon became the commodore of the Larchmont Yacht Club, a very exclusive club located in Larchmont, New York, just over the border in Westchester County. The boats competed mainly on Long Island sound and Caldwell was the talk of the area. His father would no doubt have been proud of the man his son had become; Caldwell was the very epitome of what a rich young man should be like. He had graduated from Yale and must have cut a handsome figure indeed with his J-shaped sideburns that connected to his full moustache as he sailed his yacht the "Dauntless."

Caldwell Hart Colt

While Caldwell was sailing the Dauntless, which interestingly, had first been owned by James Gordon Bennet, the founder of the New York Herald, the newspaper that had written so unkindly about Caldwell's uncle John, Samuel, the son of Caroline Henshaw, who was rumoured to be the illegitimate son of the late Samuel Colt had arrived from Germany and was now working at the Colt Armoury.

Elizabeth was said to have been fond of the boy and when he decided to marry a young woman from Georgia, Elizabeth not only paid for the wedding but gave the couple a house on the Armsmear estate.

Elizabeth may well have felt justified in believing that she could spend the remainder of her life, without suffering any more pain than she had already endured, but sadly, she would have been wrong.

In mid-January 1894, Caldwell, now thirty-five, had been in Punta Gorda, Florida, sailing his winter boat the "Oriole" and news reached Armsmear that he had been found dead aboard the schooner under what appeared to be mysterious circumstances.

Elizabeth had been planning the twenty-fifth anniversary of the Church of the Good Shepherd, but now, she had to plan instead for the burial of her fifth and last child.

Caldwell had a reputation for holding lavish parties on

his boats and as with any rich young bachelor there were always rumours of affairs and intrigue. Following his death, rumours of suicide and murder were rife and one hinted that he had fallen overboard and drowned during a drunken party.

Elizabeth however, had been informed that Caldwell had experienced a severe attack of tonsillitis and, as a complication of that ailment, had suffered from heart failure. Caldwell's best friend, William Prime, who had been with him when he died, wrote a letter to the Hartford Courant hoping to end the rumours.

"These rumours are absurd and pure fabrication. If to be so published it will grieve Mrs. Colt very much and ought to be promptly denied. When we went into dinner at 6 o'clock on the night he died, I told everyone that Colt was dying and he died two hours later."

After enduring the pain of losing her husband and daughter, Elizabeth had built a church, now she would build the "Caldwell Colt Memorial House." The building was designed by architect Edward Potter, who Elizabeth coxed out of retirement for the project, and it was completed in 1896. In todays money the building cost around thirty million dollars and remains one of Hartford's great buildings.

With no one to pass the great Colt empire onto, Elizbeth sold the company to a group of Connecticut capitalists with the one proviso that the company must always bear the Colt name. The company was sold for a sum that translates today as hundreds of millions of dollars.

Elizabeth had Samuel and the children exhumed from Armsmear and reburied at Cedar Hill Cemetery just up the road in 1894.

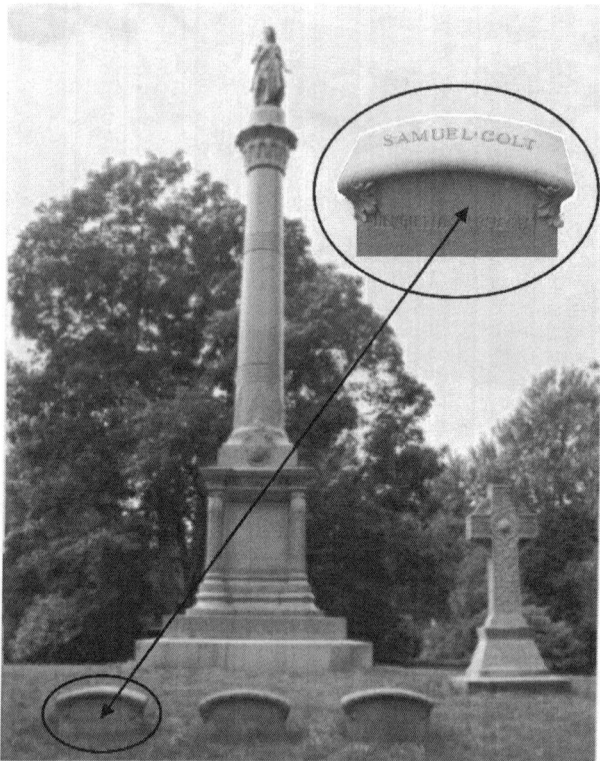

Colt's family memorial
at Cedar Hill Cemetery

The family memorial at Cedar Hill Cemetery that was commissioned by Elizabeth was designed and constructed by Hartford architect and sculptor James G. Batterson. The monument is an Egyptian Revival design (a popular funerary style in the mid-19th century) and is constructed of grey granite quarried in New London and rose-coloured syenite, a compound rock, from quarries in the north of Scotland. At 40 feet high, the monument incorporates pyramidal reliefs, a lotus flower capital, and the Colt family arms and is topped with a bronze statue modelled by sculptor Randolph Rogers.

Elizabeth herself died on August 23rd 1905, just shy of her 79th birthday, at the home of her niece, whom she had been visiting in Newport, Rhode Island.

In her will, Elizabeth left a great deal of money to a great many people. She asked that Armsmear become a home for widows and orphans of deceased clergymen of the Protestant Episcopal Church, together with as many impoverished but refined and educated gentlewomen as the building would support.

The church of the Good Shepherd was left the equivalent, in today's money, of twenty-eight million dollars as a budget to maintain it in a state of complete repair at all times.

Summing up

In reading about and researching Samuel Colt, I've come to realise just what a complicated man he was, clever, religious, self-motivated and determined by nature, I don't think many would have managed to carry on and achieve their childhood ambition in the face of quite so much opposition and adversity.

It is understandable that later in life he came to bear a bit of a grudge against those who had opposed him, be it from jealousy or just lack of foresight. He undoubtedly made as many enemies as friends along the way and had his many dissenters, both then and now.

Some people now condemn Colt simply because he was a gunmaker. Personally, I think it is important to look at the character and beliefs of a man within the context of the times they were living in. I think it's unfair to judge someone according to the beliefs and moral standards of today if they were living in a day and age when things were looked on from a completely different perspective.

Guns are a controversial subject and of course it's possible to live these days without bearing arms and the vast majority of people do, but back in Colt's day things were very different. Even in the bigger cities, of both Europe and

America, police enforcement was unreliable and the streets were full of robbers, thugs and other undesirables. The majority of law-abiding citizens would carry a weapon of some sort for defence, and a club, a sword-stick or pocket pistol were the most common.

Life on the American frontier was different again, and would have been impossible without guns, they were an important and essential tool for survival in every household.

Every man on the frontier would have needed to be proficient, at least in the use of a rifle. Boys would have learnt to shoot as soon as they were big enough to hold a gun, and by the age of twelve they would have been expected to play their part in putting meat on the family table and to take their place beside the men in times of attack by hostiles. In that regard, Samuel Colt was simply providing an essential tool.

People accuse Colt of being corrupt in his business dealings because he wasn't averse to bribing people and made gifts of presentation arms to some with a view to gaining orders, and it's true, he did, and the odd white lie about delivery times may have passed his lips. Maybe you view that as a flaw in his character and cause to censure, or maybe you just except that a lot of business was done that way back then, and probably still is. Maybe he was so frustrated with how difficult it was to get his invention excepted, that he was willing to go to any length to get a deal.

The most damning criticism that's made against him, however, is the charge of being in favour of slavery, but I don't think that really holds water if you examine the evidence.

It's true that the only time I can see that he referred to slavery in letters to his father, he condemned it on the grounds of the detrimental effect it had on the slave owning population of the south, rather than on the slaves themselves.

It is also true that some articles were written, siting how useful a revolver would be in the event of a slave uprising, and Colt did nothing to object to these articles. He seems to have been careful not to comment either way, a sale is a sale.

It is also clear that he was a lifelong Democrat and supporter of his good friend, Stephen Douglas, the Democratic candidate who was defeated by Abraham Lincoln in 1860, and was an advocate of a policy known as, "popular sovereignty."

Popular sovereignty is a doctrine rooted in the belief that each citizen has sovereignty over themselves. Citizens may unite and offer to delegate a portion of their sovereign powers and duties to those who wish to serve as officers of the state, depending on the officers agreeing to serve according to the will of the people. In the United States, the term has been used to express this concept in constitutional law. It was also used during the 19th century in reference to a proposed solution to the debate over the expansion of slavery. The proposal would have given the power to determine the legality of slavery to the inhabitants of the territory seeking statehood, rather than to Congress.

This would seem to indicate that Colt's views on slavery were very much, on the fence, and that he had no moral objection to it, however, in a letter written to a Scottish acquaintance, Andrew T. Allen, on Dec. 6, 1849, Colt, speaking of the slavery he had seen in Turkey wrote that, *"the condition of slavery there (in Turkey) I find practically abhorrent."*

It should also be remembered that Colt gave out abolitionist pamphlets to his employees on Dec. 30, 1860, and arranged for an abolitionist minister to deliver a sermon on the subject to the entire workforce, hardly the action of a pro-slaver.

One must also bear in mind the fact that Elizabeth, his wife, was the daughter of a Episcopalian rector, and they would certainly have been abolitionists and it is unlikely that he would have approved the marriage of his daughter to a man who supported slavery, and equally unlikely that the marriage would have been as strong as it obviously was, if the couple had held different view on the subject.

And lastly, you only have to look at the radical steps he

took to ensure the wellbeing of his workforce, he was at the forefront of the movement to improve working conditions.

I think the truth is that Samuel Colt believed that slavery was wrong, but in the early days when he was struggling to build his business, he was reluctant to let his personal feeling interfere with sales. You may call this a weakness in his character, but before he was rich and famous, his opinion would have meant nothing anyway.

Samuel Colt was a man of his times, who was in many ways ahead of his time.

Chapter Fourteen

The Inventions

The Revolver:

The idea of a gun with a revolving cylinder wasn't a new one by any means, indeed Fig 1 shows a six shot snaphaunce revolver from circa 1616 that is in The Royal Armouries Collection, London.

One of the most popular guns of the early to mid-nineteenth century in America was the Allen pepperbox revolver shown in Fig 2. The Allen was a double action revolver, that is to say that pulling the trigger both cocked and fired the weapon, making it the fastest firing pistol of the day.

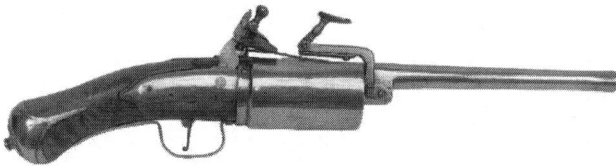

Fig 1
Six shot snaphaunce revolver 1660
Courtesy of The Royal Armouries Collection

The pepperbox had its problems however, it was difficult to aim because of the positioning of the hammer on the top of the gun, and the fact that quite a lot of pressure was needed on the trigger because of the double action. There was also a tendency for more than one chamber to fire at a time. Mark Twain, who was well acquainted with the gun, wrote several humorous comments about his "Allen, Fig 2"

Fig 2

An Allen pepperbox revolver

Courtesy of The Metropolitan Museum of Art

Colt's idea was to move away from the concept of multiple revolving barrels and produce a weapon with a single barrel and a revolving cylinder along the same lines as the Collier revolver shown in Fig 3.

In the case of the Collier revolver, it was necessary, after firing a shot, to cock the lock, rotate the cylinder by hand and then close the cover of the flash-pan over the primer. The frizzen was mounted on the right of the barrel, as would be found on a standard flintlock pistol. The rotation of the cylinder permits the touch-hole, which has a sliding cover, to line up with the frizzen. In percussion hand-rotated guns, these actions were reduced to two, cocking the pistol and rotating the cylinder.

It is surprising that, although many Collier flintlock revolvers were later converted to percussion, Collier himself appears to have stopped making revolving pistols when the percussion era came in and returned to civil engineering.

Fig 3

Collier flintlock revolver circa 1800

Courtesy of Ian McCullum, Forgotten Weapons

It was the invention of the percussion cap around 1820 that made Colt's revolver a practical weapon. The percussion cap is a small cylinder of copper or brass with one closed end and it resembles a miniature top hat.

Inside the closed end is a small amount of a shock-sensitive explosive material such as fulminate of mercury. The percussion cap is placed over a hollow metal "nipple" at the breech end of the chamber. Pulling the trigger releases the gun's hammer and that strikes the percussion cap and ignites the explosive primer. The flame travels through the hollow nipple to ignite the main powder charge in the chamber.

To start with, Colt produced three handguns, a belt pistol, a holster pistol and a pocket pistol, along with two rifles, Figs 4 and 5. All featured a revolving cylinder and were manufactured at the Paterson plant. The early Colt revolvers had a folding trigger that was deployed when the gun was cocked and were of single-action design, meaning that the gun had to be manually cocked before it could be fired and pulling the trigger performed one action, it discharged the weapon.

The revolving mechanism consisted of a lever or pawl that was attached to the hammer and operated upon a toothed ratchet cut on the base of the cylinder, causing it to rotate as the hammer was moved to full cock. A spring attached to the pawl, pressed against the frame of the pistol, keeping it in close contact with the cylinder during cocking.

Fig 4
A Colt Patterson revolver
Courtesy of The Metropolitan Museum of Art

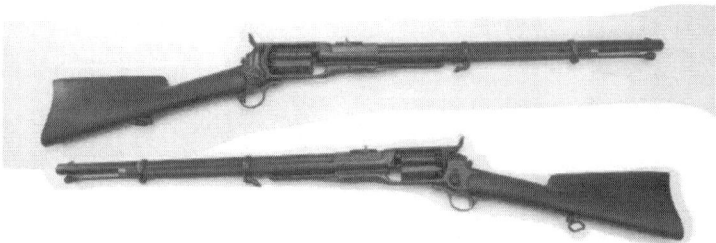

Fig 5
Colt's carbine

Another part of Colt's mechanism was the cylinder-bolt or stop that secured the cylinder in the firing position. The cylinder-bolt was fixed see-saw fashion upon a screw passing through the gun frame. The front end was shaped to fit into a corresponding series of slots cut into the surface of the cylinder and was held in place by a light spring, Fig 6.

As the hammer was raised, it lifted the back end of the cylinder-bolt, depressing the front and allowing the cylinder to revolve freely until the hammer reached full-cock, when the bolt was released and snapped back into position, once again locking the cylinder in place. When the trigger was pulled and the hammer fell, the hind part of the cylinder bolt, which was made of spring steel, was pressed slightly to the side allowing the hammer to pass, after which it sprung back into place ready for the next shot.

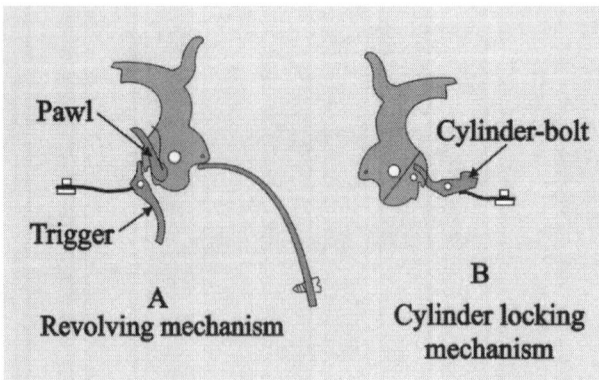

Fig 6
Colt's revolving mechanism

The first Paterson Models (1836–1838) required partial disassembly for loading and had no definitive provision for safely carrying the revolver with all chambers loaded.

To load the revolver, the shooter would have to:

1. Draw the hammer to half-cock to free the cylinder for removal and rotation.
2. Push the barrel wedge from right to left until it stops against a retaining screw.
3. Pull the barrel and then the cylinder off the central arbor.
4. Fill the individual chambers with powder leaving enough room to seat a lead ball.
5. Using a special lever tool or the arbor, seat balls in the chamber.
6. Replace the cylinder, barrel, and wedge and with the hammer at half cock, and place a percussion cap on each tube using the Colt-designed capping tool.

The revolvers came with spare cylinders, Fig 7, and the practice of the day was to carry spare cylinders loaded and capped for fast reloading. Period users had few qualms about this practice even though it presented a real hazard of accidental discharge if the caps were struck or the cylinder dropped.

Fig 7
Boxed Patterson showing the spare cylinder

Routine carry modes included leaving the hammer in the half-cock position, lowering the hammer to rest on a capped chamber, downloading by one cylinder, or lowering the hammer between the chambers of the cylinder. The first two options were (and are) extremely dangerous. Later Colt revolvers had a notched hammer that would fit over an intermediate safety pin located between cylinders on the back of the chamber when all cylinders were loaded, thereby obviating contact of the hammer with the percussion caps until the single-action hammer was intentionally cocked.

In 1839, a hinged loading lever and capping window became standard for new revolvers and was retrofitted to the older designs. So modified, the revolvers could be loaded without disassembly. When the Paterson revolvers with loading levers finally reached Texas in 1842, Texas Ranger Captain John Coffee Hays was very pleased that his ranger companies could now reload from horseback.

In one reported incident, Captain Jack Hays and fifteen Texas Rangers, armed with Colt's revolvers, defeated seventy-five Comanches, killing over thirty of them. Even if one allows for some exaggeration on the part of the brave Rangers, it is nevertheless strong evidence for the worth of Colt's gun.

When Captain Walker, who had been with Hays in the Comanche encounter helped Colt redesign his gun, the result was the Colt Walker pistol shown in Fig 8.

Although Colt himself died in1862 the company he founded has continued to manufacture firearms until the present day.

Fig 8
The Colt Walker

Horace Smith and Daniel Wesson patented a rim-fire cartridge and obtained rights to produce a gun with a bored through cylinder, heralding in the day of the modern cartridge firing revolver, and giving Smith and Wesson a monopoly on breech loading pistols until 1869.

It is strange that Colt's company didn't start making cartridge firing guns until four years later in 1873, when they produced the Model P. Fig 9.

I am sure that if Samuel had still been alive, a new cartridge firing Colt revolver would have been designed and stockpiled ready to be delivered to suppliers on the very day the Smith and Wesson patent expired.

Imaged by Heritage Auctions, HA.com

Fig 9
Colt model P 1873

The Waterproof Cartridge

Paper and linen cartridges had been used for years to speed up the loading process of muzzle loading weapons, it meant that a measured amount of powder and a ball or bullet could be loaded into the barrel at the same time. The problem was that they were still just as vulnerable to damp as loose powder, Fig 10.

Samuel Colt, along with Willian T. Eley developed a cartridge that used tin foil instead of paper or linen, making it much less susceptible to damp.

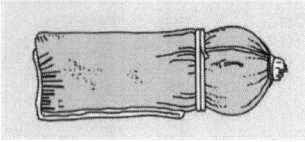

Paper Cartridge   Linen Cartridge

Fig 10

During manufacture, after it had been filled with powder, the end of the tinfoil case was crimped into the base groove of the bullet. which was then greased and this produced a waterproof cartridge. The cartridge was then enclosed in a paper wrapper, from which it could be easily removed before loading, Fig 11.

Fig 11

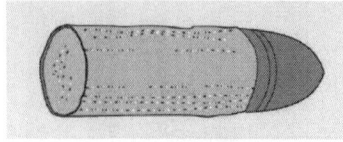

Tin foil Cartridge

The image on the right of Fig 11 is the waterproof tin-foil cartridge, the image on the left shows it in its protective case with a tape to pull the cartridge out.

Due to the shape of the bore of the nipple in Colt's revolvers, the flame from a percussion cap would pierce the tin foil and ignite the powder, without the need to tear open the foil. The drawback was that an undesirable residue was left in the cylinder due to the foil not being entirely consumed by the explosion.

During 1843 the army gave Colt an order for 200,000 of the tinfoil cartridges packed 10 to a box for use in muskets.

Submarine Battery

I have already described the incident at Ware pond when Samuel Colt attempted to blow up a raft by means of an underwater explosion and how this was achieved by use of a copper wire insulated with tar that conveyed an electric current to the charge. It is not actually clear whether Colt used a galvanic cell or a Leyden Jar to generate the electric current but most accounts suggest a galvanic cell.

Colt was very secretive about his submarine battery and it is unclear exactly what his mine looked like, but Fig 12 is a representation of how it may have looked, based on mines used during the Civil War.

Fig 12

Underwater mine

The idea behind the submarine battery is to protect a harbour from attack by enemy warships before the harbour itself is in range of the enemy's guns, using underwater mines.

There are two major problems to overcome in doing this. First, you have to have a long enough cable to convey the electric charge to the mine, from a place of safety and concealment, and second, you need some way of knowing exactly when to set off the explosion. The mine needs to explode when a ship is on top of it, or it is of no use whatsoever.

One way to do this, of course, would be to put marker buoys over the mine positions, but the obvious drawback to that is that the buoys would also be visible to the enemy ships, that could then navigate to avoid them.

Colt's method for achieving this, although greatly shrouded in secrecy, appears to have employed what Colt himself referred to as "torpedo towers."

The Torpedo Tower was basically a tall building with an opening at the front near the top, overlooking the area of the river that was mined. An angled mirror would then project an image of that section of the river onto a viewing table or platform mirror on which the locations of the mines would be marked.

The viewing table mirror would have electric terminals embedded in it, whose positions would correspond to those of the mines.

The operator would see the approaching ships reflected onto the platform and could detonate the right mine by connecting the appropriate terminal when an enemy ship passed over it, Fig 13.

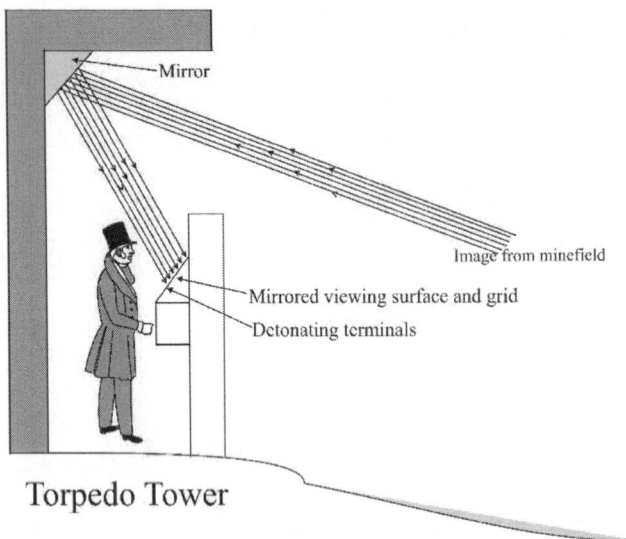

Fig 13
Torpedo Tower

In the end Colt was unable, perhaps because of his almost paranoid secrecy, to convince the necessary authorities to adopt his submarine battery and this failure may have set America's underwater warfare capability back by several years.

In addition to this, Samuel Colt always claimed to possess a further secret, which many of his friends believe he took with him to his grave, but so reticent was he on the subject, that even to this day it is unclear whether this secret related to his explosive compounds, or to how they were arranged, or to his method of ascertaining exactly when they should be set off. Some speculate that, rather than using a Torpedo Tower, as he insisted he did, he had some way of making vessels that touched his mines communicate their position by some means of telegraph.

Appendix

1. The Minié bullet:

Muzzle loading muskets were not very accurate because the ball had to be a loose fit in the barrel for loading. Rifles had a tight-fitting ball or bullet in order to take the spin imparted to it from the rifling grooves inside the barrel, but this made them difficult to load and the loading process took more time, which was undesirable on a battlefield.

For that reason, rifles were often loaded with a loose-fitting ball that was wrapped in a greased "patch" of linen. This patch made the ball easier to load and served to impart the necessary spin, but having to wrap the ball in the patch prior to loading still took too much time.

The search was on to find a way of making a lose ball a tight fit after it was loaded and the breakthrough came when, Captain John Norton experimented with an expanding bullet in 1823.

The idea was that an elongated bullet should have a cavity in the base and that the force of the charge itself would cause the bullet to expand to fit the bore and take spin from the rifling, but his idea was not taken up.

In France, Captain Delvigne also decided that a loose-fitting bullet with a hollow base would be expanded by the force of the charge and fit the bore tightly, but it was another Frenchman who would give his name to the system of gas expanding projectiles.

Claude Etienne Minié refined the shape of Delvigne's bullet and in 1849 he added a small iron cup, designed to be driven into the base of the bullet on discharge, thus ensuring a uniform expansion on all sides. The cup however, was found to be a hazard, sometimes parting from the bullet and leaving the muzzle separately and endangering other soldiers in the vicinity. It was also found to be unnecessary.

The British determined that a slightly redesigned bullet worked well without a cup, although they backtracked somewhat and added a boxwood plug anyway. If nothing else, it did help to prevent any damage occurring to the bullet before loading. At the same time, the Americans reached the same conclusions. James Henry Burton, Assistant Master Armourer, designed a bullet that needed no plug of any kind and it was quickly adopted by the government.

It was Burton's bullet design, and one can only speculate as to how irked he was, that the Americans insisted on calling it a "Minié Ball," after Claude Minié.

It is of no consequence but interesting to note that,

Delvigne, who first looked at the possibility of an expanding hollow-based bullet, receives no credit in the public's mind for originating the system. Burton and the British designer who produced projectiles that actually saw use, are seldom mentioned. Minié, on the other hand, whose system was defective and only saw experimental use, became a familiar word in America.

2: John Colt's Death

The sentence of death imposed on John Colt for the murder of Samuel Adams sparked off renewed debate about the rights and wrongs of capital punishment. Lydia Maria Child, a forthright and outspoken abolitionist in the fight against slavery, was also a powerful voice in the battle to end the death penalty.

The day after John Colt's death she wrote:

"Heart, head and conscience are all in battle army against the savage diatoms of my time. By and by, the laws of love, like oil upon the waters, will calm my surging sympathies and make the current flow more calmly, though none the less

deep or strong. But today, do not ask me to love governor, sheriff or constable, or any man who defends capital punishment. I ought to do it; for genuine love enfolds even murderers with its blessing. By tomorrow, I think I can remember them without bitterness; but today, I cannot love them; on my soul, I cannot."

She also wrote:

"We were to have had an execution yesterday; but the wretched prisoner avoided it by suicide. The gallows had been erected for several hours, and with a cool refinement of cruelty, was hoisted before the window of the condemned; the hangman was all ready to cut the cord; marshals paced back and forth, smocking and whistling; spectators were waiting patiently to see the die game. Printed circulars had been handed abroad to summon the number of witnesses required by law: "You are respectfully invited to witness the execution of John Colt". I trust some of them are preserved for museums. Specimens should be kept as relics of a barbarous age, for succeeding generations to wonder at. They might be hung up in a frame; and the portrait of a New Zealand Chief, picking the bones of an enemy of his tribe, would be an appropriate pendent".

Horace Greeley, who agreed with the jury's verdict, wrote in the Tribune:

"What has been the influence of the Punishment of Death in this case? What moral effects have been produced by its existence? Have we not seen the community divided with regard to the justice of the sentence? Not from compassion to criminals but from regard to the community, whose sympathies and whose feelings are so unhealthily excited by public executions, whose abhorrence of crime and reverence for laws are confused and disturbed by these deeds of legal butchery, we demand the abolition of the Punishment of Death."

A piece that was originally published anonymously but has since been attributed to Walt Whitman, reads:

"But a few short summers since, John C. Colt was sporting round the hearth of fond parents in all the gaiety and glee of child-like innocence. And but a few months since, he was threading the devious path of life with all the pride and ambition of self-confident youth. Who that might have seen him at either period of life would not have been appalled at the thought that his career was to be in crime—in blood—in double murder? Had he been told as he walked abroad erect among

his gay companions that such would be his fate, how would his eye have kindled and his bosom swelled with deep and irrepressible indignation? And yet, young men of New York, he did it all. He knew not himself, and was not master of his fierce and desolating passions.

Let us be admonished by this terrible example. Let us ask—Do we know ourselves any better than he knew himself? Do we comprehend, and have we the fixed moral principle, the high moral energy, to control the fearful volcano of human passions whose maddened fires roar and blaze within our bosoms?"

As well as arousing debate about the death penalty John Colt's death gave rise to numerous rumours, one of the most common being that he had in fact escaped. Various different methods of escape were suggested, amongst which was the theory that he had escaped during the confusion caused by the fire wearing his new wife's dress, and that he had then been smuggled aboard a ship bound for France. The body of a pauper convict is supposed to have been substituted for his, to be found stabbed in his cot.

Among those who accepted that John Colt had committed suicide there was a great deal of speculation as to how he had acquired the knife. Almost all of those who visited

John in his cell were suspected at some time or another and some even suggested the knife had been concealed in the clothing of the infant brought to the cell by Caroline Henshaw.

Some enemies of Samuel Colt put it about that John had been persuaded to commit suicide by his brother in order to spare his family the ignominy of the gallows.

Another enemy of the Colt brothers, John Gordon Bennett published an article suggesting that John's last-minute wedding to Caroline Henshaw was a sham. It speculates that they were in fact already man and wife, indeed Caroline often called herself Mrs Colt.

Most people believed that John had married Caroline for honourable reasons but Bennett suggested otherwise.

"Circumstances that have recently come into our possession," wrote Bennett, *"have persuaded me that Colt and Caroline were actually married in Philadelphia before the murder of Adams took place in this city. After this deed was committed, it became necessary that she should be used as a witness, and knowing that her testimony could not be received as the wife of Colt, she was introduced as plain Caroline Henshaw, and for the purpose of carrying out the deception as originally practiced, the marriage ceremony was again performed, in order to blind the eyes of the world to the previous transaction."*

3: Samuel, Uncle or Father?

The possibility that Caroline's child was actually Samuel Colt's son has already been mentioned, as has the fact that he would look after the boy and his mother. His efforts on their behalf began shortly after John's death, when he sought help from a woman who had long proven herself a friend, Lydia Maria Child. Lydia Child and Samuel Colt had met through a mutual friend, Lydia Huntley Sigourney who had helped Samuel re-join Hartford society.

Samuel had approached Mrs. Child to solicit her aid in finding suitable living arrangements for his brother's widow and the infant boy he was determined to "treat as if he were his own son."

We know of Sam's visit from a letter that Child addressed to her friend John Sullivan Dwight on December 1, 1842 Mrs. Child wrote:

"Mr. Colt's brother has been to see me and consult with me about her (Caroline). He says he believes her to be a modest, worthy girl; that she never formed any other connection than that with his unfortunate brother ... He says

he feels it a duty to do more for her than feed and clothe her;
that he ought, as far as possible, to throw a protecting influence
around her and the child whom he shall in all respects treat as
if he were his own son. "I want to educate her," says he; "to
put her under influences that will make her a judicious mother
for my brother's son. But where shall I find a suitable place? I
have thought of a country clergyman's family; but she would
be pointed at in a country village, and she would have little
chance to improve intellectually; and in most cases there would
not be that entire forgetfulness of her peculiar situation, which
is desirable." I at once thought of the West Roxbury
Community, and mentioned it; at the same time telling him that
you were so much crowded that I thought it not very likely you
could take her. I had other fears than those of your being
crowded. I thought you might perhaps fear the "speech of
people." But, my dear friend, this is a real case of a fellow
creature fallen among thieves, wounded and bleeding by the
wayside. If she were a loose woman, I would be the last to
propose such a thing. But I think she is not. She is, as I believe,
an honest confiding young creature, the victim of a false state
of society. She is almost heart-broken, and longs for seclusion,
soothing influences, and instruction how to do her duty. If you,
with your large and liberal views, and your clear perception of
human brotherhood, if you, at West Roxbury, reject her, where,

in the name of our common Father, can I find a shelter for her poor storm-pelted heart? ... My soul is on its knees before you, to receive this poor shorn lamb of our Father's flock. I am in agony, lest you should not listen to my supplications, for somehow or other, though a stranger to me, God has laid her upon my heart.

Mr. Colt seemed to leave the arrangements to me; but I thought his idea was to have her board with you for a year, doing what conveniently she could, consistently with the care of her child; and you to make such deductions from the price of board as her labours were worth; and if you found her a useful and pleasant inmate, to make such after arrangements about the education of the child, &c as should seem proper".

Historical records do not indicate whether Mrs. Child succeeded in securing a yearlong residency at Brook Farm for Caroline and baby Sam.

Samuel and his brother James continued to look for a suitable home for Caroline and her son and in the end, it would seem that they ended up in Germany.

Colt historian William Edwards wrote that Samuel Colt had married Caroline Henshaw (who later married his brother,

313

John) in Scotland during 1838, and that the son she bore later was Samuel Colt's and not his brother John's. In a 1953 biography about Samuel Colt based largely on family letters, Edwards wrote that John Colt's marriage to Caroline during 1841 was a way to legitimize her unborn son as the real father, Samuel Colt, felt she was not fit to be the wife of an industrialist and divorce was a social stigma at the time.

In Colt's will, he left his "nephew" a great deal of money and some accounts record that Elizabeth Colt and her brother Richard Jarvis contested it in probate court. In court, it is claimed that Caroline's son Samuel, produced a valid marriage license showing that Caroline and Samuel Colt were married in Scotland during 1838 and that this document made him a rightful heir to part of Colt's estate. There is however, no surviving record of such a marriage or real evidence for it.

4 Caldwell Hart Colt

Caldwell Hart Colt was the only one of Samuel Colt's children to survive him. He attended Yale University and followed in his father's footsteps by becoming a gunmaker and designing a double barrel rifle in 1879. He was a keen yachtsman and served as vice commodore of the New York Yacht Club in 1888 and as commodore of the Larchmont Yacht Club from 1892 to 1893.

In mid-January 1894 Caldwell was sailing his winter boat the "Oriole" in Punta Gorda, Florida Caldwell was found dead aboard the schooner under what appeared to be mysterious circumstances.

Elizabeth had been planing the twenty-fifth anniversary celebrations of the Church of the Good Shepherd, but instead found that she had to make preparations to bury her last remaining child.

There was nothing left for Elizabeth, except to have built the "Caldwell Colt Memorial House" as the parish house for the Church of the Good Shepherd.

6 Factory Fire

Description of the fire at Colt's factory from,
Armsmear, The Home, The Arm, And The Armoury Of
Samuel Colt. A Memorial,

*For one who has written concerning the Armory with
such affectionate minuteness as in the foregoing description, of
its rise, progress, and multifarious departments, it is a sad task
to chronicle its downfall, plunged in an ocean of fire. Yet thus
it must be.*

On the 5th of February, 1864, the writer of this paper was railroading from the West to Milwaukee. He met a friend from Marquette, on Lake Superior, and was asked, "Have you heard the news?" and on answering "No," was told that Colt's Pistol Factory was destroyed. He felt the pang which pierces in a personal bereavement, a pang which was renewed the next summer when he rambled about the ruins, stones fire-blackened and ready to crumble through heat, machines tortured into strange shapes, and walls tottering to their fall among weeds, with which nature was already beginning to mantle the desolation. The scene was such as we associate not so much with the new world as with the old, where stones, themselves to ruin grown, are gray and death-like old.

On that February morning the Armoury labours commenced at the usual hour of seven, and all was well for an hour. Very soon after eight o'clock, some of those engaged in the upper story, noticing smoke near its ceiling, gave an alarm and ran upstairs. Others followed, with hose from the hydrant, which they pointed at a black vapor that was streaming out of the drying-room; but the water, from some unexplained cause, came not until too late. The drops, which at this moment could have extinguished all, would have been worth their weight in gold.

A little fire is quickly trodden out, which, being suffered, rivers cannot quench. No water came, but fire did. Thus long it had smouldered among the patterns in the drying-room. It now burst forth, drove the men from the attic, and caught the roof beneath the dome. The attic floor was soon burned through, so that coals fell on that of the third story, which, composed of yellow pine, and soaked in oil from the drippings of machinery, at once spread the fire every way faster than a man could walk. Thus, it fared with the second story, and thus with the lowest. Within one hour after the first smoke was discovered, the roof, with its dome and rampant colt, its supports having been consumed, fell in, re-enforcing the flames that were already all-conquering beneath. Each floor was an acre of flame, all machinery covered with oil, all wood saturated with it, ten thousand gallons in reservoirs, besides other combustibles, augmented the fury of the conflagration, already uncontrollable.

Men did what they could. The steam gong, which had been heard fifteen miles, was heard through the city sooner than any cry or bell. The fire companies with their steamers were at once in motion. But the water in cisterns was scanty, and it must be brought more than seven hundred feet from the river; besides this, the hose burst more than once. Yet, had there been none of these untoward accidents, it is by no means certain that the best possible play of the engines could have stopped the raging element, after it had gained full headway, sooner than it was in fact arrested, namely, midway between the old and the new factories. The combustion was most intense and rapid, till there was nothing more in the old factory to burn. Thus, perished the whole original erection of Colt, the chief basis of his fortune and fame.

The further progress of the flames was arrested mainly through the herculean efforts of the armorers themselves. An interested observer of the scene writes: "As they saw wall after wall weakened by the heat, and falling beneath the play of the engines, they rose in their strength to do battle. But for them, doubtless the whole, instead of the half, of that noble pile of buildings, the mechanics' pride, had been laid low. Each taking the bucket provided for him, to remove from face and hands the marks of toil before going to his home at noon and night, and forming lines from the hydrants to the roof, in the part known as the New Armory, they determined to save it. Some upon the slate roof, so near to the burning mass that it seemed impossible humanity could endure it longer, amid the stifling smoke, and the groans of the steam gong, almost human in its wailing, beside the falling walls of their home for many a year, did these brave men labour with the might that only affection can give; they loved their chief, who had gone from them forever, and they willed that their hands should save his monument from destruction.

Thus, one line passing down the empty buckets as the full ones came up, at times almost compelled, by the fearful heat of the atmosphere about them, and the almost burning slate roof under their feet, to abandon all to the fierce fire, they at length drove it back inch by inch, until at length, though worn and weary, they came down victorious, triumphant.

God bless those brave, true men, now and for aye! Their efforts, by saving the New Armory, enabled the company in three days to go on with the completion of their contract with the Government, without asking for any extension of time.

The office might have been saved, had the bridge uniting it to the main edifice been cut away in season. When a tardy effort was begun in this direction, it was thwarted by someone shouting from the crowd that there was a ton of powder in the cellar.

Owing to the machine-drawings and other valuables in the office, its destruction, though it was not a large building, swelled the loss by some hundreds of thousands. The lower story of it was in fact saved; but the main struggle of the engine-men was to rescue the new building, and in this they succeeded. One loss, much deplored, was that of certain unique machines, tricks to show the extent of human brain, the models of which also perished, for executing certain delicate and important tasks most quickly, perfectly, and cheaply.

Some costly things went to ruin because the windows were grated, the workmen locked in, and a principal door for a time impossible to open. Among these, some (as the screw machines) were the only specimens of their class this side the Atlantic, and not to be at once replaced. The value of the machines lost was estimated at $800,000, that of the stock at half that sum, and the insurance covered about one-third of the amount destroyed.

One man was burned to death; several others, hanging out of high windows by their hands, could not reach the ladders with their feet. They must have perished, had not their friends bethought themselves and been strong enough to lift those ladders up to their feet. More than eight hundred men were in one moment thrown out of work, while the injury to the Arms Company and to the country was aggravated by the check given to pistol-making in the very crisis of a war when they were more than ever needed.

In this regard a significant anecdote is related respecting a speculator in New York, who, the minute he saw the telegram that the Armory was on fire, hurried to the largest pistol dealer there, and bought up his whole stock before that dealer learned the news.

The greatest fire-plague that has ever smitten Hartford cannot be forgotten by any who witnessed it; it is conceivable only by those whose own eyes have beheld a conflagration equally vast. Instead, therefore, of declaiming upon the catastrophe in stilted prose, we shall better recall it, or paint it, in the words of the fire-scene in Schiller's Song of the Bell, a portraiture which genius has so drawn that, as long as fires burn, men will never cease to recognize its truthfulness, thus verifying the sage maxim of Aristotle, that poetry utters universal truth, and hence is more truthful than history.

"An instrument of good is fire,
With man to watch and tame its ire;
And all he forges, all he makes,
The virtue of the flame partakes;
But frightfully it rages, when
It breaks away from every chain,
And sweeps along its own wild way,
Child of nature, stern and free.
Woe, if once, with deafening roar,
Naught its fury to withstand,
Through the peopled streets it pour,
Hurling wide the deadly brand!

Eager the elements devour
Every work of human hand.

Hark! what tumult now
Rends the sky!
Lo! the smoke up-rolling high I
Flickering mount the fiery shafts;
Where the wind its wild wave wafts,
Onward through the street's long course
Rolls the Elaine with gathering force;
As in an oven's jaws, the air
Heated glows with ruddy glare;
Falling fast the rafters shatter,
Pillars crash and windows clatter.
Through the air in graceful bows
Shoots the watery stream on high.
Fierce the howling tempest grows;
Swiftly Horne upon the blast,
Rides the flame, devouring fast;
Roaring, crackling, it consumes
All the crowded armoury rooms;
All the ratters blaze on high;
And, as if 't would tear away
Earth's foundations in its flight.

On it mounts to heaven's height,
Giant-tall!
Hope hath all
Man forsaken; helpless now
He to heavenly might must bow,
Idly musing o'er his fall,
Wondering at his work laid low."

The resourceful spirit of the Firearms Company was shown in that their workmen in the unburned half of their establishment, on the second secular day after the conflagration, were at their labours again as if nothing had happened. It is further manifest in their now rebuilding just on its old foundations, and more incombustible, whatever fire had thrown down. Thus is also fulfilled a prophecy in which, writing of the Armory three years ago, then in its pristine perfection, we indulged, namely: "No matter though his manufacture be burned to ashes, and not one stone be left on another, his invention would rise as from the pyre of the Phoenix, and clothe itself in a new, perhaps a more noble embodiment."

Regarding the origin of the fire, opinions will perhaps never coincide. Some traced it to rebel emissaries, such as burned Western steamers and New York hotels; others were convinced that cotton waste, used in scouring attic machinery, had been left in the drying-room; others judged the heat of the steam there had become so great as to ignite the dry wood.

Had Col. Colt survived until the day of the fire, insurance men tell us that the loss of the company would have been four hundred thousand dollars greater, inasmuch as he never insured his property. On the other hand, had he still lived, the fire might not have occurred. His quick-eyed, persistent vigilance, for which nothing was either too vast or too minute, might have kept the water-pipe in working order, or deterred the scourer from leaving his waste in a fatal spot, or have hurried away the dried wood before it began to burn. After all, what might have been is beyond our judging.

"There's a divinity that shapes our ends,

Rough-hew them how we will."

Well is it said, "Higher spirits may discern the minute fibres of an event stretching through all time and space, and hanging on the remotest limits of the past and of the future, of the near and of the distant, where man sees no more than a point, isolated and unconnected. The changes, then, which would flow from the change of any antecedent, however trivial, who shall not confess it beyond his conjecture?"

7 Elisha K. Root

The death of Elisha K. Root, on the 5th of July, 1865 was a loss, not just to Colt's company but also to the world of inventions and industry. He was born in Hampshire County, in the State of Massachusetts, May 5th, 1808. He was educated at a district school for four months in the year, until he was fifteen years old, when he became apprentice in a machine-shop in Ware, where he worked as a "bobbin boy" for eight months in the year, from the time he was ten years old until he began his apprenticeship.

After serving his apprenticeship in the machine-shop in Ware, he worked as a machinist in various factory villages, and among them at Stafford, Connecticut, and at Chickpea Falls, Massachusetts, returning occasionally and for brief periods to Ware.

On one of these visits he saw, for the first time, Samuel Colt, experiment in blowing up a raft on Mill Pond by an underwater mine. In 1832, Root moved to Connecticut, and became connected with the Collins Company, in Collinsville. The originator of that successful company writes:

"He came here and offered his services in 1832, a young man about twenty-five years of age, without any recommendation, except a remarkable head and eye, indicating

a man of more than usual mental ability. He called himself a machinist, and commenced work at a turning-lathe in our repair-shop. It was not long before his superiority became manifest, and he was appointed overseer of that shop, and in a few years was virtually overseer of all the shops, though not appointed superintendent by our directors until 1845. He invented several useful machines for facilitating our work, some of which were patented. He never manifested anxiety to obtain large compensation for his services, but was content to bide his time. In 1845 he was offered the situation of 'master armorer' in the United States Armory in Springfield, and about the same time he received two offers from large manufacturing concerns in Massachusetts, with very liberal compensation, which resulted in our giving him increased pay to remain with us. In 1849 Col. Colt made him very liberal offers, more than we could afford to pay, but he was satisfied with his compensation here, and would probably have remained, if I had not advised hm to accept this offer as a matter of duty to himself and his family. He was with me seventeen years, and O knew him intimately. He was not only a superior mechanic, with great inventive faculties, but he was a man of excellent judgment, and great caution and prudence, which cannot be said of inventors generally.

He was also a deep thinker on most subjects that interest men of science and thought. He was a man of great simplicity and purity of character, a very modest, unassuming man, and yet very decided and firm. He was a very conscientious man, so that all who had business with him were impressed with his strict honesty and integrity. He was a man of liberty, in every sense of the word. He was averse to display of any kind and despised all sham. He was a very superior man and had few equals. Such a man is a great loss to any community. Anything I could say would be deemed faint praise by those here who knew and loved him "

When employed by Colt invented and patented too many machines to mention here and improved many more. He must be counted among the world's most productive inventors.

8 Presentation pieces

Samuel Colt was in the habit of having special presentation pieces made for important individuals and here are some examples of the type of quality of these pieces, together with some thank you letters from the recipients.

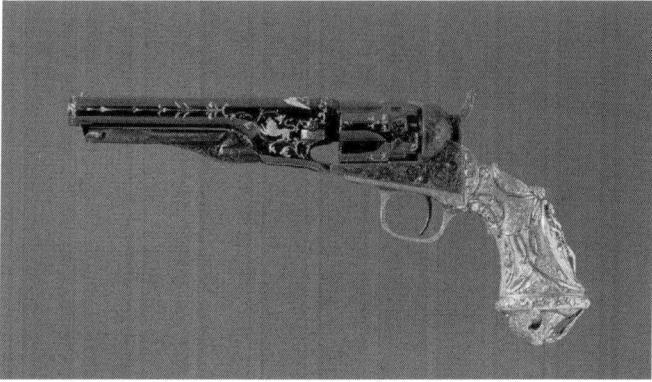

Colt 1862 Police model revolver in steel, copper and gold
unknown recipient
Courtesy of the Metropolitan Museum of Art

Letter from Lord Palmerston:

Broadlands, January 6th 1852

Dear Sir

I have many apologies to make to you for having so long delayed, amidst a heavy pressure of business, to thank you, as I now beg to do, for the beautiful revolver which you have been so good as t send me. It is indeed an admirable specimen of ingenuity of invention, and of perfection of finish. I shall preserve it not only as a valuable memorial of that great exhibition which brought the nations of the world into such friendly contact, but as an evidence of the kindly feeling on the part of our brethren in the United States, to the maintenance and increase of which I attach such great importance; and I trust that for many a long year to come the people of our two countries may know nothing of each other's weapons except through such acts of courtesy as that for which I am now making my acknowledgments.

I hope on my return to town to have the pleasure of making your acquaintance, and of repeating my thanks to you in person.

I have the honour to be, Sir, yours faithfully,

Palmerston

Colt third model dragoon pistol c 1853
Unknown recipient
Courtesy of the Metropolitan Museum of Art

Letter from Aimable-Jean-Jacques Pélissier, Marshal of France. (Translation)

General Quarters, august 20th 1855

Colonel

His Grace the Duke of Newcastle has had the goodness to send me the two revolving pistols which you had the kindness to offer me.

I accept your present, and thank you for having sent these beautiful arms, to which you have given so ingenious a fabrication and a remarkable perfection.

They have been exceedingly admired by those of our officers who use firearms.

I am much touched at this cordial politeness, and pray you to believe in my distinguished consideration.

Letter from the Major King of Siam:

Bangkok, Siam, January 24th 1859

Sir

I have great pleasure in the receipt of your kind present of powerful and beautiful firearms, being our revolving rifle and the four pistols of various size, kept in good order in the box covered with crystal, through the introduction and the care of Commodore Perry, who is now, I have heard dead.

Whereas Reverend Mr. S. Matlen, the American officiating council, will return to his home, I have liberty to intrust to his care a golden snuff-box, a silver water-pot, a silver plate with stand, a silver cigar-case, richly gilt, for your acceptance. I hope they will be the token of my remembrance; and I beg to express my very heartful thanks for your kindness towards me, and beg to present to you one of my cards, out of respect to you. I have the honour to be,

Your good friend

Somdet Phea

Paramendr

Maha Mong Kut

P. S. I will write you again on another opportunity, regarding your manufactures.

Letter from G. Garibaldi   (Translation)

Gino, January 15th 1860

Noble Colonel Colt

As an adopted citizen of the grand Republic, and proud to labour in the all-embracing cause of the peoples, I thankfully, in the name of my country, accept your sympathetic and generous gift.

The arrival of your arms will be haied among us, not merely as material aid dispatched by a man of heart to a people who fight for their most sacred rights, but as a subsidy of moral potency from the great American nation.

I am affectionately your servant,

G. Garibaldi.

Poem

On The Death Of Samuel Colt

Lydia Huntley Sigourney

And hath he gone, whom late we saw
    In manly vigor bold?
That stately form and noble face
    Shall we no more behold?
And now of the renown we speak
    That gathers round his name
For other climbs beside our own
    Bear witness to his fame;

Nor of the high inventive power
    That stretched from zone to zone,
And 'neath the pathless ocean wrought,
    For these to all are known;
Nor of his love his liberal soul
    His native city bore,
For she hath monuments of this
    Till memory is no more;

Nor of the self-reliant force
    By which his way he told,
Nor of the Midas-touch that turned
    All enterprise to gold
And made the indignant River yield
    Unto the osiered plain, -
For these would ask a wider range
    Than waits the lyric strain; -

But choose those unobtrusive traits
       That dawned with influence mild,
When in his noble mother's arms
       We saw the noble child,
And noted, mid the changeful scenes
       Of boyhood's sports or strife'
That quiet, firm, and ruling mind
       Which marked advancing life.

So, onward as he held his course
       Through hardship to renown,
He kept fresh sympathy for those
       Who cope with fortune's frown -
The kind regard for honest toil,
       The joy to see it rise,
The fearless truth that never sought
       His frailties to disguise -

The lofty mind that all alone
       Gigantic plans sustained,
Yet turned boastfully away
       Frome fame and honors gained;
The tender love for her who beat
       His home with, angel-care,
And for the infant buds that rose
       In opening beauty fair.
Deep in the heart whence floes this lay
Is many a grateful trace
Of friendship's warm and earned deed
Which naught can e'er replace;
For in the glory of his prime
The pulse forsakes his breast,
And by his buried little ones
He lays him down to rest.

And thousands stand with drooping brow
Beside his open grave,
To whose industrious, faithful hands
The daily bread he gave –
The daily bread that wife and babe
Or aged parent cheered,
Beneath the pleasant cottage roofs
Which he for them had reared.

There's mourning in the princely halls
So late with gladness gay –
A tear within the heart of love
That will not dry away –
A sense of loss on all around,
A sigh of grief and pain
"The like of him we lose today,
We may not see again."

Index

Other books by Colin Holcombe

Non Fiction

A History of Firearms: ISBN 978 1787233300

How to Restore Antique Furniture: ISBN 1 86126 008 3

Marquetry Techniques: ISBN 1 86126 0571

An Introduction to Woodwork: ISBN 1 86126 321 X

The Care and Repair of
Antique Furniture: ISBN 978-1516899081

Cabinet Making: ISBN 978-1787233393

Antique Furniture Restoration
An Illustrated Guide: ISBN 978-1787233522

Party Tricks Magic and Puzzles: ISBN 978 1787233928

Fiction

First Time Hard   ISBN 978 1787233362

The Moving Finger Writes   ISBN 978 1787233379

Murder Out of Bounds   ISBN 978 1787233386

Murder Under the Hammer   ISBN 978 1787233447